A Passion for God

The Mystical-Political Dimension of Christianity

Johann Baptist Metz

Edited and translated, with an introduction by
J. Matthew Ashley

PAULIST PRESS
New York / Mahwah, N.J.

The publisher gratefully acknowledges use of the following materials: "Theologie als Theodizee?" by J. B. Metz in *Theodizee: Gott vor Gericht,* edited by Willi Oelmüller, copyright © 1990. Reprinted by permission of Wilhelm Fink, München. "Theologie versus Polymythie oder kleine Apologie des biblischen Monotheismus," by J. B. Metz in *Einheit und Vielheit, XIV Deutscher Kongreß,* edited by Odo Marquard, copyright © 1991. Reprinted by permission of Felix Meiner, Hamburg. "Vorwort zur 5. Auflage," by J. B. Metz in *Glaube in Geschichte und Gesellschaft,* copyright © 1992. Reprinted by permission of Matthias-Grünewald, Mainz. Excerpts from *Kirche nach Auschwitz: mit einem Anhang: für eine anamnetische Kultur,* by J. B. Metz, copyright © 1993. Reprinted by permission of Katholische Akademie, Hamburg. J. B. Metz, "Vorwort" and "Religion, ja—Gott, nien," from J. B. Metz and T. R. Peters, *Gottespassion,* copyright © 1991, Verlag Herder: Freiburg, Basel, Wien.

Cover design by Calvin Chu

Library of Congress Cataloging-in-Publication Data

Metz, Johannes Baptist, 1928–
   [Essays. English. Selections]
   A passion for God : the mystical-political dimension of Christianity / Johann Baptist Metz : edited and translated, with an introduction, by J. Matthew Ashley.
     p. cm.
   Includes bibliographical references (p.).
   Contents: The new political theology—On the way to a post-idealist theology—Theology as theodicy?—Theology versus polymythicism—Do we miss Karl Rahner?—Karl Rahner's struggle for the theological dignity of humankind—The church after Auschwitz—Theology and the university—Monotheism and democracy—A passion for God.
   ISBN 0-8091-3755-0 (alk. paper)
   1. Christianity and politics—Catholic Church. 2. Liberation theology. 3. Theodicy. 4. Catholic Church—Doctrines. I. Ashley, James Matthew, 1958– . II. Title.
BX1793.M47213   1997
261.7—dc21

                                                  97-36614
                                                        CIP

Published by Paulist Press
997 Macarthur Boulevard
Mahwah, New Jersey 07430

Printed and bound in the
United States of America

Contents

iii

iv   CONTENTS

In Place of a Foreword:
On the Biographical Itinerary
of My Theology

My younger colleague and translator Dr. Matthew Ashley and the publisher at Paulist Press have asked me to write a foreword to this collection of some of my more recent essays. In place of the usual foreword, I would like briefly to show how the itinerary of political theology has been a reflection of my life. I hope these biographical notes will illuminate the background out of which individual contributions to this volume have arisen, and I offer them as an expression of gratitude to the translator.

I

Toward the end of the Second World War, when I was sixteen years old, I was taken out of school and forced into the army. After a brief period of training at a base in Würzburg, I arrived at the front, which by that time had already crossed the Rhine into Germany. There were well over a hundred in my company, all of whom were very young. One evening the company commander sent me with a message to battalion headquarters. I wandered all night long through destroyed, burning villages and farms, and when in the morning I returned to my company I found only the dead, nothing but the dead, overrun by a combined bomber and tank assault. I could see only dead and empty faces, where the day before I had shared childhood fears and youthful laughter. I remember nothing but a wordless cry. Thus I see myself to this very day, and behind this memory all my childhood dreams crumble away. A fissure had opened in my powerful Bavarian-Catholic socialization, with its impregnable confidence. What would happen if one took this sort of remembrance not to the psychologist but into the Church? and if one did not allow oneself to be talked out of such unreconciled memories even by theology, but rather wanted to have faith with them and, with them, speak about God?

This biographical background shines through all my theological work, even to this day. In it, for example, the category of memory plays a central role; my work does not want to let go of the apocalyptic metaphors of the history of faith, and it mistrusts an idealistically smoothed out eschatology. Above all, the whole of my theological work is attuned by a specific sensitivity for theodicy, the question of God in the face of the history of suffering in the world, in "his" world. What would later come to be called *political theology* has its roots in this speaking about God within the *conversio ad passionem*. Whoever talks about God in Jesus' sense will always take into account the way one's own preformulated certainties are wounded by the misfortune of others.

II

So now I must say something about political theology, which I formulated in the mid-sixties and for which consequently I am held answerable. From the start, Dorothee Sölle and Jürgen Moltmann have been particularly supportive of me in this undertaking, and so this theological endeavor was always understood to be an ecumenical project—ecumenical in the sense of an indirect ecumenism, a collaboration in a public contest for the sake of God and the world. Now let me give a few reflections on the path this political theology has followed.

1. My experiences with the so-called Paulus-Gesellschaft, which in the early sixties was dedicated to bringing Christians

and Marxists into dialogue, and particularly with Ernst Bloch and members of the Frankfurt School, "politicized me out of" the existential and transcendental enchantment of theology.[1] I have always understood the debate with Marxism to be really a debate with the social-critical dramatization of the theodicy theme. I did not want politics and political culture to be spared theodicy's perspective, as every kind of pragmatism recommends. Of course, I also wanted to articulate this theme differently from Marxism: as always and absolutely a question about others' suffering as well as one's own, about the suffering even of one's enemies, and about suffering in the past, which not even the most passionate struggle on the part of the living can touch and reconcile. This way of bringing together politics and theodicy had and continues to have a high price, for it is continually made an object of derision by political pragmatists and by political utopians as well, both those outside and inside the Christian world. But how, except through this theodicy-outlook, can one save political life from pure political Darwinism, which cares not if it is implemented by a pragmatic straight path or laden with dialectical hesitations?

2. If I judge correctly, the atmosphere of 1968 (often disparaged today) had one effect above all on me: it drove out the all-too-pliable language of the historicity of faith and confronted my theology more and more clearly with history itself, with history that bears a name as catastrophic as that of Auschwitz. Again and again since then I have asked myself why one sees and hears so little in our theology of such a catastrophe, or of the whole history of human suffering. Could it possibly be that we have used categories for the theological interpretation of history that are too strong, categories that too quickly cover over every historical laceration and allow the sensorium for danger to atrophy? Does theology really heal every wound? At the time, Auschwitz worked like an ultimatum for me. Since then the supposedly weak categories of memory and narrative have played an ever greater role for me, are even able to express the terror of the logos of

theology, and help me focus on the anamnestic culture that has developed in Jewish history.

3. Since the late sixties there have been two impulses of the Second Vatican Council that I have tried above all to defend and strengthen under the banner of political theology. There was the impetus for believers to walk on their own two feet ("Only the one who walks upright can also bend the knee willingly and give thanks cheerfully.") and, seminally present in this, the first indications of a revision of the relationship of my Church to the political Enlightenment. But above all there was in the council the first outline for a movement out of European monocentrism and into a culturally polycentric global church with painful social divisions. Encounters with my friends in the international journal *Concilium* were particularly fruitful in this regard.

During my stays in the United States it became ever clearer to me that there is a growing conflict of cultures or civilizations within Catholicism in the Western, so-called first world, a clear alienation and lack of connection between Roman Catholicism on the one hand and the religious-political traditions of the Anglo-Saxon world on the other. Yet for me the new theological challenge became that of drawing in the non-Western world, the so-called third world. This exposed the logos of theology to social suffering and misery as much as it did to the suffering that comes from being culturally and ethnically different in a world and world church dominated by the West. I will never forget my encounters with my friends in liberation theology in Latin America and my experiences in the base communities of these nations.

Since encountering these and other cultures as well, I have worked to formulate a concept of theology that, while it recognizes the post-modernists' legitimate suspicion of universalistic approaches, does not collapse into a sheer relativization of cultural worlds. I have striven to do this by stressing a respect for and obedience to the authority of those who suffer. For me this authority is the only one in which the authority of the sovereign God is manifested in the world for all men and women.

III

I will stop here. The leitmotif of this biographical path is quite probably the *memoria passionis,* the remembrance of the suffering of others as a basic category of Christian discourse about God. This entails the theodicy question, continually taken up under a temporal signature and dramatized in a social-critical way—a question that for me is never silenced or taken care of by the Christian message of redemption. In every thing there is always a loud, or at times a silent, cry. This is what led me not long ago, for example, to ask Jürgen Habermas in a friendly way whether it has really been settled once and for all that the meaning of human language is rooted in communication and not, perhaps, in that cry. There are for me questions that may be directed back at God, the God of Abraham, Isaac, and Jacob, the God of Jesus. Here though are questions for which I have a language, but no answers. And I have made them my own as a prayer: Why, God, suffering? why sin? Why have you made no provision for evil?

One can see how important this is for my theology by the fact that I have interpreted from its perspective my incomparable teacher Karl Rahner, who hardly ever spoke himself of theodicy and negative theology—and I would not want to take up such a way of speaking about God apart from him. In 1984, the year of his death, I wrote that "Karl Rahner has never interpreted Christianity as the happy conscience of an advanced bourgeois condition that has been purged of every endangered hope, every vulnerable and stubborn longing....Through it all there remained in him a longing, which I never felt to be sentimental, nor something that stormed the heavens, but which was much more a hushed sigh of the creature, like a wordless cry for light before the face of God shrouded in darkness."

Johann Baptist Metz

Introduction: *Reading Metz*

I. THE MYSTICAL POLITICAL ELEMENT
IN METZ'S THOUGHT

Some ninety years ago Friedrich von Hügel described religion as a complex interaction of three elements or modalities: the historical, the intellectual and the experimental.[2] The historical or historical-institutional element is the mode in which religion presents itself as something objectively *there*, factual and unchanging. It includes the person, words and deeds of the founder (insofar as they can be historically secured, elaborated on and passed down), as well as the rites, practices and institutional structures that attempt faithfully to pass on the essence of the founder's activity. The intellectual element, with synthetic and analytic moments, seeks system and coherence, not only within the worldview that the religion presents in its historical-institutional aspect, but with other perspectives on reality as well. Finally, in its experimental or mystical-volitional element, "religion is rather felt than seen or reasoned about, is loved and lived rather than analyzed, is action and power, rather than external fact or intellectual verification."[3] From this perspective the vitality of religion as a social phenomenon, as a force undergirding the development and creative activity of mature human subjects, depends upon the creative interplay and integration of these three elements, overcoming again and again (both in individuals and in the broader group) the tendency of each element to dominate or suppress the other two. The history of a religion, as long

7

as it remains a living force, is the history of the continual effort to forge anew this creative union in multiplicity.

Whatever its value as a general phenomenology of religion, the model aptly describes Roman Catholicism. It also provides a helpful heuristic device for reading the works of Catholic theologians (at least) in this century, including Johann Baptist Metz. For Catholic theology this century is defined by two events: the suppression of the modernists at its beginning and, in its second half, the profound renewal of Catholic intellectual life, with its epicenter in the Second Vatican Council—from the laborious preparation in the decades preceding it, to the ongoing task of interpreting and handing on its heritage. The first moment, using von Hügel's model, represents the suppression of the intellectual element by the historical-institutional; the second shows the profound reinvigoration of a religion in general, and of its intellectual element in particular, that follows when the three elements interact creatively.

The generation of theologians who completed their training around the time of the council, a generation that includes Johann Baptist Metz, had as its task not so much preparing the ground for the council or even harvesting its first fruits, but rather dealing with the new challenges that confront the church as it approaches its third millenium. For, as von Hügel would have insisted, the creative synthesis forged at the council must be continually forged anew; fidelity to the council must mean fidelity to a unity in multiplicity. The key to reading Metz is to grasp his profound commitment to the task and understand the many ways he has tried to bring together the historical-institutional, intellectual and mystical-volitional (for him, mystical-*political*) dimensions of Catholicism. Even less than his great mentor and teacher, Karl Rahner, does Metz have a closed, mechanical system. Rather, his theological work is better described in terms of a cluster of diverse elements which, like an astronomical cluster, has no one fixed star around which it revolves, but rather is constituted by the complex interactions between its many components.[4] These components can be grouped under von Hügel's three elements.

a. Metz's Catholicism: the Historical-Institutional Element

The historical-institutional modality of Metz's religion is German Catholicism. His commitment to the institutional church and its historical traditions is evident in his vocation to the priesthood, his work for the (then) West German Episcopal Synod and his concern for religious life. Metz's Catholicism is not simple, however, but resolves into a complex and shifting field of elements. While it is distinctively German, Metz has in fact become increasingly aware of the broadly catholic character of Catholicism. As the decades passed, and particularly during the nineteen-eighties, Metz came to broaden his commitment to include more explicitly the church of the third world, and he followed Rahner in pressing for a truly global, polycentric church. As he himself states, this "irruption" of the third world into the church's consciousness has been one of the challenges that has shaped the new paradigm of political theology.

Yet it is important to tarry with the local character of Metz's Catholicism. Johann Baptist Metz was born on August 5, 1928, in the small Bavarian town of Auerbach. The Catholicism in which he was reared has had a lasting impact on him. As he himself says of it:

> One comes from far away when one comes from there. It is as if one were born not fifty years ago, but somewhere along the receding edges of the Middle Ages. I had to approach many things slowly at first, had to exert great effort to discover things that others and that society had long ago discovered and had since become common practice.... [F]rom a point quite removed I had to work my way into the academic and social discussion fronts, had to learn to comprehend things that supposedly my theology and I had already discovered and comprehended long ago, had to gain access to phenomena that my contemporaries seemed to master through clichés: enlightenment, pluralism, emancipation, secularization, the critique of capitalism and

Marxism. And I had to learn how difficult and problematic it was to connect these parameters of contemporaneity…with that religion already so familiar to me before I had begun reflecting on it.[5]

Metz ascribes his own "noncontemporaneity" to this Catholicism, to this "way of looking at things," this "psychological life-rhythm."[6] Here we find a striking but also productive tension between Metz's commitment to the historical-institutional reality of his church and his intellectual commitment to modernity. As much as Metz is committed to the ideals of Enlightenment, he never fully condemns Catholicism's hesitancy at entering the modern age. As much as he criticizes nineteenth-century Catholic theology for sealing itself off from the intellectual and cultural debates raging in Europe, it is not because it failed to "keep up with the times," but because it demonstrated a failure of nerve, a failure to trust that the substance of tradition was up to a thorough confrontation with modernity. Thus, while he argues against a sectarian mentality of intellectual self-isolation in Christian faith and theology, he nonetheless finds their proper contribution to society and academy in large measure to be a particular kind of resistance, a carefully measured but engaged *non*-contemporaneity with the modern scene, a willingness to tarry with and defend notions and symbols (like those related to sin and guilt and, above all, apocalyptic ones) that are too quickly dismissed by modern, progressive consciousness as archaic, precritical or psychologically immature.

The key point here is that Metz takes this position not out of *hostility* to the Enlightenment, but in the conviction that these religious resources are necessary if modernity is to be saved from its own dialectical self-destruction. Metz's Germany, like that of his philosophical contemporary, Jürgen Habermas, is the Germany for which the Enlightenment is an "unfinished project."[7] For them the Enlightenment is still something to be saved and realized. This commitment is rendered particularly problematic because Metz's Germany is also the Germany of National Socialism. The Weimar Republic expired when he was

INTRODUCTION: READING METZ 11

only five years old, and the rest of his childhood was spent during the Third Reich's lock-step march to destruction. For Metz, as for so many who lived through those dark years, one of the great questions is how the Germany of Goethe, Kant, Beethoven and Planck, could become the Germany of Hitler, Himmler and Eichmann. Finally, then, Metz's Germany is the Germany of Auschwitz; while he argues forcefully that it is not just German Catholics who must reckon with a church *after Auschwitz,* its impact on him as a German Catholic marks one of the great interruptions that continually invades his thinking.[8] Any reading of Metz must reckon with this complexity of the historical-institutional dimension of his religious commitments. It is a richly textured fabric—woven from his rural Catholic upbringing, the ambiguous history of European Catholicism's relationship to modernity, the complicity or failure of German Catholicism under National Socialism, and his growing consciousness of the church's global catholicity and the challenges deriving therefrom—that shapes all his work.

b. Metz's Catholicism: the Intellectual Element

Metz was introduced into the intellectual element of religion through an extended apprenticeship in transcendental Thomism. To use Metz's own words, that approach "is characterized by the attempt to appropriate the heritage of the classical patristic and scholastic traditions precisely by means of a productive and aggressive dialogue with the challenges of the modern European world."[9] Metz mastered this approach under Karl Rahner. However much he departed from it, some of its most basic features continue to characterize his later thought: a commitment to critical dialogue with the Enlightenment, in the conviction that its *turn to the subject* can be fertile ground for Christian faith and theology;[10] a consequent focus on anthropology, on starting with the experience and action of human subjects as the proper framework for developing and legitimating theological statements;

finally, a concern with human historicity, with temporality as a constitutive dimension of human existence.

In 1963 Metz took a position in fundamental theology at the University of Münster and began moving rapidly away from the specific formulations of this approach. But the underlying commitments remained. He tells us that he shifted to the Kant of the second critique and of the philosophy of history, moving into dialogue with the second phase of the Enlightenment.[11] Becoming increasingly aware of the aporias in modernity, in part as he grappled more and more with the "Germanness" of his Catholicism, he read widely from other critical defenders of Enlightenment like Max Horkheimer, Theodor Adorno, Ernst Bloch and Walter Benjamin. And Metz reads these not just as modernity's deconstructing critics, as he does the postmodernists (whom he ferociously opposes), but rather as thinkers who would save the best ideals of the Enlightenment by saving it from itself. Thus he has continued a "productive and aggressive dialogue with the challenges of the modern European world." In addition, however much he emphasized the social constitution of persons and pressed for a more radical understanding of human historical involvement than the notion of *historicity* would provide, he insisted that "political theology…must elaborate itself as a theology of the subject."[12] This was the project he completed (at least to his own satisfaction) in the pivotal work of his career, *Faith in History and Society*. There he developed an understanding of the subject in terms of categories of memory, solidarity and narrative, which can profitably be understood as an alternative set of *existentialia* to those presented in Heidegger's or even Rahner's existential-transcendental analytic of human existence.[13] Finally, he worked out his own understanding of temporality as an alternative to the one implicit in the Rahnerian notion of historicity; this understanding of temporality, which drew on the work of Ernst Bloch and Walter Benjamin, allowed Metz to articulate the incipient apocalyptic sensibility that defines for him the "mystical" element of Christianity.[14]

c. Metz's Catholicism: The Mystical-Political Element

Finally then, and most importantly, Metz's work cannot be understood without grasping how it construes Christianity's mystical-volitional element, which becomes for Metz its mystical-*political* element. This element shows up in bold relief when we consider one of the greatest enigmas of Metz's theological career: his relationship to Karl Rahner. That, after attempting to mold Rahner's brand of transcendental Thomism to deal with his emerging concerns, Metz abandoned it in favor of a new "political theology," is undeniable.[15] That he considered, and still considers, Rahner to be not only his theological master but his "father in faith," is well attested by the two essays on Rahner included in this volume. Why did Metz strike out on his own instead of continuing his collaboration with Rahner, who, for his part, was quite cognizant of the new challenges looming for a postconciliar church and worked energetically in the last two decades of his life to respond to them?

The answer lies with what Metz praises most highly about Rahner, that is, the ability to bring together spirituality and theology, to render theologically a "mystical biography of the ordinary, average person."[16] Rahner held himself accountable to everyday believers, particularly those beset by the doubts engendered by the precarious existence of Christian faith in the secularized, scientific-industrial societies of European modernity. He made their doubts his own, and responded to them with the full force of his penetrating grasp of the resources of the Catholic doctrinal tradition. But, as Metz himself insists, he did not do this by "pour[ing] interpretations of religious experience 'from above' into bewildered souls; rather, [his approach] worked because it was an invitation to a journey of discovery into the virtually uncharted territory of one's own life."[17] Rahner invites us into a personal journey that is at the same time (to cite one of Rahner's favorite medieval theologians) an itinerary of mind and spirit into God. Metz argues forcefully, and correctly in my view, that this is the deepest source of Rahner's greatness.

But what if the concerns of the everyday believer are those of

Metz's generation, which grew up under the dark shadow of National Socialism and had the task of rebuilding their lives and culture after Auschwitz? What if the reality that contextualizes and threatens modern belief is not just, or even primarily, that of secularization and unbelief, but the horrifying worldwide prominence of inhuman suffering, the existence of crucified peoples?[18] Metz begins his own preface to this volume with the memory of his experience as a young soldier shattered by the impersonal brutality of modern war, and has identified therein the "dangerous memory" that has driven his theological journey. What happens when such remembrances become more the rule and less and less the exception?

What sort of mysticism would correspond to *those* types of experience? For Metz, it does not center on the Rahnerian, apophatic and essentially neo-Platonic presence to God as absolute, holy Mystery, with its tradition reaching back through the Rhineland mystics to the Cappadocians, Origen, and Clement of Alexandria. Rather, Metz picked up on another strand of Christian spirituality, one that is much more engaged or irritated by the presence of evil in creation, as well as by the lack of (or perhaps better, by the still outstanding) response on the part of God. This is the tradition of apocalyptic spirituality, reaching back through figures like Thomas Müntzer and Joachim of Fiore, and finally—as Metz avers—to the biblical figure of Job.

This form of presence to God takes the form of protest, of insistent questioning: How long, oh Lord? This insistent turning of one's question toward God finally contextualizes suffering as a *suffering unto God*.[19] This mysticism, which he also calls a mysticism of open eyes (open particularly to perceiving the suffering of others, both living and dead), is at the heart of Metz's theology, just as Rahner's mysticism of God as absolute, holy Mystery is at the heart of his. It informs his advocacy of an apocalyptically bounded time, in opposition to evolutionistically unbounded, limitless and deadening time, as well his insistence on the primacy in Christology and ecclesiology of the *memoria passionis*. This mysticism defines for him the primordial, authentic way of being human in a world and church that lives inescapably after Auschwitz. He has pressed for it not only within Christianity, but in society at large and in the academy, as a remedy for the growing forgetfulness and demise of the person as a responsible historical agent (of his or her own and others' histories) and a remedy for the decline into a gentle, anesthatized "second immaturity" (*Unmündigkeit:* that state the emergence from which is, according to Immanuel Kant, the meaning of Enlightenment). In short, if there is one of the three elements of von Hügel's typology that is most central to Metz's work, it is the mystical-political. This is also true of Rahner; the difference lies in the precise texture of the "mystical" for these two theologians.

Before we specify the difference more precisely, let us first consider how the complex emergence and interaction of these three elements has driven Metz's theological itinerary. In the first phase of his work (1950–1963), Metz operated (however uncomfortably) within the paradigm of transcendental Thomism, and tried to mold it to express the as-yet-unnamed mystical stance that had grown out of the complexity of his German Catholic experience. After 1963 he became increasingly dissatisfied with this endeavor. Perhaps due to moving out of Rahner's direct influence and perhaps as well to the turbulent sixties, which enabled Metz's own dangerous memory to emerge as far more normal than before, Metz began trying out new intellectual tools, particularly from the revisionary Marxist thought of Ernst Bloch and of the Frankfurt School. Very likely it was in reading Bloch and Benjamin that Metz first came up against an overtly apocalyptic stance toward time and became aware, especially from Benjamin, of the lost or neglected resources of Judaism.[20] Although he had been moving away from Rahner's theology throughout the sixties, it was not until he fully incorporated this apocalyptic understanding of temporality, along with the corollary understanding of reason as memorative or anamnestic reason, that Metz's intellectual pilgrimage ended. To the extent that the result is a *system,* it is found in *Faith in History and Society.*

What then of Metz's relationship to Rahner? I have suggested here that the key difference derives from their different spiritualities. Rahner certainly was aware of the new challenges facing the church and humanity in general on the threshold of the second millenium. However, while he refashioned his theology by plunging ever more profoundly into the spiritual fountainhead from which he had drawn from the outset of his theological career, Metz shifted to an apocalyptic spirituality, a mysticism of suffering unto God, as he named it. Rahner and Metz are profoundly alike in their creative fidelity to the church, and in their insistence that theology be fashioned as mystagogy, as an intellectual project that initiates one ever more deeply into the mystery of discipleship. In this they could, and did, remain deeply respectful friends. It was over the status of apocalyptic symbols that they disagreed most strongly, yet even here they understood and appreciated each other. This is not just due to their deep friendship. After all, these two spiritual traditions—Christian Neoplatonism and apocalypticism—have interacted (to be sure, often battled) with one another throughout the history of Christianity.

The spirituality of Ignatius of Loyola, to which Rahner was committed as a Jesuit and which Metz learned by association, is an apt device for making this clear. The heart of Ignatius' spirituality is the *Spiritual Exercises,* made up of four parts or weeks. For Rahner the hermeneutical key for interpreting the whole was the fourth week, with its strongly Neoplatonic "Meditation to Obtain the Love of God" and the transformation that follows upon finding God in all things.[21] For Metz, as well as for Jesuits like Sobrino or Ellacuría, a different sort of transformation provided the key. It was found in the third week of the *Exercises,* in which one meditates on Jesus' passion, or in the meditation on sin during the first week. I believe that Ellacuría's paraphrase of the colloquy that ends the latter exercise describes the spiritual center of Metz's theology as well:

> I only want—I am trying not to be too demanding—two things. I want you to set your eyes and your hearts on these peoples who

are suffering so much—some from poverty and hunger, others from oppression and repression. Then (since I am a Jesuit), standing before this people thus crucified you must repeat St. Ignatius' examination from the first week of the *Exercises*. Ask yourselves: what have I done to crucify them? What do I do to uncrucify them? What must I do for this people to rise again?[22]

The power of this spirituality is witnessed by the liberation movements and theologies that risk this sort of transformation. Ultimately, Rahner was too good a Jesuit not to hear the voice of the third week in the work of his student. Metz, for his part, never denied the importance of the hope and confidence engendered by the resurrection and the sense of God's presence in all things. He only wanted to make sure that these did not drown out the still present, all too audible, cries of the crucified in our world. Finally, then, both understood at a deep level that, just as the weeks in the *Spiritual Exercises,* their distinctive mystical-political positions are part of a greater whole; both are initiations into the breadth and length and height and depth of the love of Christ, which surpasses all knowledge (including that of theological systems). In and because of this, each always listened to and learned from the other with the utmost seriousness, and even love, that obtains between kindred spirits.

II. THE ESSAYS

The following essays are presented in order to make available in English previously untranslated works by Metz from the eighties and nineties. The first two essays are programmatic, representing Metz's own understanding of what his theology is about, and the directions he has taken in the past two decades. The next two take up more the intellectual dimensions of Metz's synthesis. In "Theology as Theodicy?" Metz presents the preunderstanding (to use the Heideggerian term) that informs his theology. The parallels and contrasts with at least the early Heidegger are worth noting. For both, thinking starts with, is interrupted by, and thereby is continually nourished by a *question*. For Metz, however, it is not the *Seinsfrage*, the question of being, that provides the initial access to a disclosure of authentic existence, but the *Leidensfrage*, the question of suffering, particularly someone else's suffering. Yet for both, the question is not there to be cleverly solved, tied up in a neatly packaged system. In Heidegger's *Being and Time* the purpose of thinking is not to "solve" the question of being, but always to clear a space for it to be asked, to combat our tendency to forget it or cover it over. For Metz, theology as theodicy should never see its goal as "solving" the question of suffering, but rather as sheltering it and clearing a space for it to irritate us, and thereby to move us to hope, to remembering the great deeds of God, to resistance, to action. In "Theology versus Polymythicism," we can note another continuity. For both Metz and Heidegger, asking their respective questions requires and leads to grasping the essence of time. In this essay Metz lays out the understanding of time that is nourished by the apocalyptic mysticism underlying his thought: *bounded* time. Evident too in this essay is a shift in Metz's interest. In the sixties and seventies the "master of suspicion" to whom Metz devoted most attention was Marx; this essay shows how his interest has shifted to the second of these masters, Friedrich Nietzsche.

Next are two essays on Karl Rahner, which show Metz's continuing admiration for his teacher and "father in faith" and also present Metz's own understanding of "agressive fidelity" to the Second Vatican Council. In the next essay, "The Church After Auschwitz," we are presented with a condensed meditation on the impact of this theme on Metz's theology. Here as always Metz insists that, to deal adequately with the Holocaust, Christianity (and Europe in general) must get beyond moral self-recrimination and halfhearted overtures; that what is required is a searching examination of the very foundations of the spiritual and intellectual worldview within which a monstrous catastrophe like this could happen and, even worse (as Metz worries), be so soon forgotten or historicized into the dustbin of history.

The last two essays anchor the book, and in some ways span

the spectrum of Metz's concerns as a theologian. In the first, "Monotheism and Democracy," Metz primarily addresses the academy and reflects on the role of religion in society. In the second, "A Passion for God," Metz's audience is the church; once again he reflects on religious orders in the church as a way of articulating his concern for the mystical-political dimension of Christianity.

In "Monotheism and Democracy," he returns to a theme that was present in his early work on political theology. In the nineteen-sixties he defined the church as an "institution of critical freedom."[23] He argued there that, just as the Enlightenment did not emerge against the spirit of Christianity but was nourished by it, so now in modernity's time of need the church could and should be a crucial antidote to the dialectic of Enlightenment. He returns to the theme in this lecture, not only incorporating more fully the category of (dangerous) memory, which he had only just begun to develop in the late sixties, but also engaging a new generation of postmodern political theorists. Ironically, in so doing Metz returns to the political theorist with whom his theology was associated three decades earlier: Carl Schmitt. The irony is that, as Metz notes, this time it is not the Right, but the fragmented and disillusioned representatives of the political Left in Europe who are now taking up Schmitt's decisionistic, totalitarian-leaning political theories, which had once legitimated the Nazi assumption of power and the march toward dictatorship. Now as then, Metz argues, neither a premodern theocratic understanding of the relationship between politics and monotheism, nor a liberal, privatizing separation of religion from politics, will do. If Christianity is to rise to the challenge of finding a new path, then in Metz's view it must forge a new mystical-political constellation out of the mystical stance of suffering unto God.

The last essay manifests Metz's enduring concern for spirituality and for religious life. As in his earlier book, *Followers of Christ,* Metz challenges religious orders to provide creative and provocative prototypes for the church's attempt to live out the mystical-political tension of discipleship.[24] One noteworthy feature of the

essay included here is his interpretation of some of the beatitudes, including poverty of spirit. As he himself asserts, his dealings with this beatitude trace out his theological journey. One of
his early and most popular books dealt with the mystical disposition from a strongly Rahnerian perspective.[25] Some twenty years
later he took it up again in *Followers of Christ,* giving what is in
many ways a presentation that is transitional between his more
clearly Rahnerian position and his mature one. In the essay "A
Passion for God," we find important elements newly incorporated into Metz's mature perspective: recovery of the lost,
repressed or distorted inheritance of Judaism; a grasp of theology as theodicy; an understanding of reason as the cognitive
dimension of a mystical suffering unto God; a statement on the
temporality of bounded time and the effect that interpretation
has on living in the world and relating to God. Metz also challenges religious orders to resist the triumph of the therapeutic in
modern culture, along with its standards of normalcy. Finally, he
discerns in religious orders the possibility of intermediate institutions that could help the church to become a truly global, multicultural (but not culturally fragmenting) and polycentric (but
not centerless) church.

These essays do not offer radically new structural elements.
On the whole, they exploit the elements worked out in *Faith in
History in Society,* although in some cases with greater clarity and
intensity. What they do offer are exemplary instances of Metz's
ability to orchestrate the three elements that von Hügel identified as crucial to the living unity and power of religion: the historical-institutional, which for Metz means understanding the
church as the bearer of the dangerous (and precisely thereby saving) memory of the passion, death and resurrection of Jesus; the
intellectual element, which Metz advocates in terms of an
anamnestic reason, a reason essentially open to interruption by
the history of suffering (a history which it denies or represses at
its peril); finally, the mystical-political: the mysticism of suffering
unto God that provokes and fructifies the political stance of
hope and resistance and of the unceasing labor required to bring

crucified peoples down from the cross. To the extent that Metz has carried on the work of his beloved teacher—and I am certain that Metz himself could think of no greater compliment—it is because he has remained faithful to the complex unity in multiplicity of these three elements.

A few words of thanks are due. First, I would like to thank Professor Metz himself, who has been very supportive of this project and agreed to write a foreword to this volume. Second, I would like to thank Professor Albert Wimmer of the Department of German Language and Literature at the University of Notre Dame for reading through and correcting my translations. The errors or ambiguities that remain are of course my own and, if anything, derive from my decisions not to follow his counsel. Fr. Lawrence Boadt, C.S.P., and Karen Scialabba, at Paulist Press, helped me negotiate (for the first time) the difficult passage from initial idea to finished book. If they were unable to make it a perfectly smooth passage, they certainly made it more humane! Finally, I would like to thank my assistant, Dr. Todd Johnson, who spent many hours helping me find English editions and citations to Metz's German footnotes.

Insofar as it falls within the purview of an editor and translator to dedicate a book, I would like to dedicate this book to Johann Baptist Metz, in gratitude for more than four decades of service to church, society, and academy. May we hear more from him in the years to come.

J. Matthew Ashley
University of Notre Dame

1

The New Political Theology: The Status Quaestionis

This volume first appeared fifteen years ago (1977).[1] A revised edition would necessarily be overburdened with additions and modifications. Hence it will be reproduced here in this fifth edition without change, and so must continue to stand on its own. In this book the first beginnings of a new political theology which date from the nineteen-sixties, are developed in terms of their relevance for fundamental theology.[2]

What is this new political theology all about in the world of theology? I will attempt a very brief answer to this question, without pretending that it will be an exhaustive one. The answer will take us beyond this text and will indicate that perspective which has since become central to this type of fundamental theology. With this in mind I ask the reader's indulgence if in the notes I limit myself to my own texts. Finally, I would like to demonstrate how my reflections on "Faith in History and Society" have continued to develop, and indicate the ways in which they have (however imperfectly) changed.[3]

What is this new political theology about, insofar as it aspires to be nothing other than theology, discourse about God in our times? It began as a sort of corrective, as a corrective to situationless theologies, to all theologies that are idealistically closed-off systems or that continually barricade themselves behind theological systems. In that sense this theology considers itself to be "postidealist."[4] It is nourished by a certain uneasiness, indeed a certain shock, an experience of nonidentity, of which I will have to speak more later. To begin with, the situation that permeates the logos of this theology, and tests its accountability, may be characterized in a formal triad that, because it is constructed quite formally, is open to misunderstanding: first, the unresolved confrontation with the processes of the Enlightenment; then, the experience of the catastrophe of Auschwitz; finally, the way in which the third world and the non-European world in general is becoming present in the world of theology.[5] But does not situating theology in this way lead to a pathetic relativization of every theological statement? No. It does, to be sure, obligate theology to take this situation into its conscience and formulate a theological concept in and from it, with all intellectual integrity. At its origins the new political theology proposed to do just that; this is what characterizes its concern as fundamental theology.

The new situation signals three irruptions or interruptions, three experiences of nonidentity at the roots of theology.

1. Social and practical questions really began intruding into systematic theology in the course of the European Enlightenment, with its primacy of practical reason in treating metaphysical questions. From the last century on, this irruption became concrete as ideology critique and the critique of religion. "Who does theology? Where and when? For whom and with what purpose?" Those were no longer peripheral questions, to be handled by some sort of theological division of labor; rather, they were constitutive questions for systematic theology. Theology, theology itself—as discourse about God—falls under the primacy of the subject, of praxis, and of alterity.[6] Only thus is it possible to discern what is meant theologically by notions like self, existence, individuation; in short, what is meant by existence in faith.[7]

By formulating the question this way, theology is not abandoning the rational responsibility of the faith and its traditions with their orientation toward truth. It is not simply evading the classical problem of the relation between faith and reason. Rather, it is trying to take into account the fact that since the Enlightenment this problem has to be treated on a new level. Faith must justify and convey itself to a reason that, for its part, wants to become practical and come into its own as a freedom of a subject, and always also as freedom of the other, which means as justice. How can theology be *fides quaerens intellectum* in this sense? The question is directed toward a *political* form of the so-called justification of faith; it lays out the starting point in fundamental theology for the new political theology, a theology which does not presume to have overcome the Enlightenment without having passed through it with open eyes. In contrast to transcendentally or communicatively oriented reason, it stresses the primacy of a reason endowed with memory, that is, an anamnestic reason. Without that knowledge of what is missing, it is not only authentic religious consciousness (that is, one oriented toward God) that would collapse into emptiness, but also the knowledge of freedom and the sense for justice.[8] The approach tries to react in an equally critical way to those contradictions and distortions that show themselves in the concrete social, intellectual and cultural processes of the Enlightenment: the threatening disappearance of the subject, a second immaturity *[Unmündigkeit]*, a new enthusiasm for myths and a religion without God.[9]

2. Late (too late?) the new political theology became conscious of the fact that it is a theology after Auschwitz, that this catastrophe belongs to the inner situation of Christian discourse about God. In no way does this mean that Auschwitz should be stylized as a negative myth. Just the opposite! To be true to the situation, *after Auschwitz* means nothing other than this: finally to accept the fact that concrete history, and the theological experience of nonidentity connected with it, have broken into theology's logos. Confronted with Auschwitz theology, theology itself—as discourse about God—cannot maintain its historical innocence: neither by the division of labor whereby the theme is diverted into Church history, nor by the usual talk of human historicity (as a sort of anthropological constant) that, because abstract, is impervious to experiences of confusion or bewilderment; nor, finally, by a faceless universalism of history, seemingly devoid of human beings, by a kind of idealism of history endowed with a consider-

able amount of apathy when it comes to the misfortune of the other or to historical catastrophe or ruin.

A theology after Auschwitz wants to draw our attention to a principle that, because of the way Christianity became theological, fell more and more into oblivion: namely, that even the logos of Christian theology is formed not simply by subjectless and historyless ideas, but rather at its very roots by a remembrancing.[10] (Not by chance did "dangerous memory" become a central category of political theology.)[11] This remembrancing cannot repress and forget, or idealistically overcome *[aufheben]* humanity's history of suffering. A new sensivity for theodicy (this will be discussed later) belongs on the agenda for theological discourse. I might even say that political theology here in Germany wants to make the cries of the victims from Auschwitz unforgettable in Christian theology, in theology itself. This would signify a farewell to every theology that closes itself off idealistically, and a farewell to the forgetfulness of the forgotten, hidden, as I see it, in its concepts of truth and of God.

In a series of contributions since then I have taken up the theme of theology and church after Auschwitz, and also the issues that follow therefrom: Christian theology, a new relationship in Christianity to its Jewish heritage, latent metaphysical anti-Semitism, and so on.[12] Here let me simply stress this: as long as we are only dealing with "religion" (whatever that means in our postmodern world, mythically enthralled and in that sense friendly to religion), we may well be able to dispense with Israel and the Jewish traditions; if however we are dealing with "God" and "prayer," then this heritage is indispensable, not only for Jews, but also for us Christians. Biblical Israel, shunned and persecuted, is and will remain the foundation for us Christians, as well as for Islam. And therefore Auschwitz continues to be a deadly assault against everything we must hold holy.[13]

3. Finally, political theology tries to take into account the irruption of the so-called "third world" and of the non-European world in general into the world of theology. It tries to do this not only pastorally, but in a strictly theological sense, as a challenge

to our discourse about God. This will direct our theological attention to a social and economic fault line in our world that cuts across the church itself: the so-called North-South conflict, which has certainly not come to an end with the cessation of the East-West conflict. Conditions that are absolutely contrary to the Gospel—the degradation of peoples, oppression, racism—become provocations to the very heart of its message. They call for the formulation of Christian discourse about God under categories of resistance and transformation. Because of this, political theology began almost from the outset to speak of the church as an "institution of the socio-critical freedom of faith" and of an ethics of transformation that would correspond to this theological approach.[14] Of course, this transformation—which becomes *liberation* in liberation theology[15]—includes the concept of the capacity for guilt and the necessity for conversion of all historical subjects. This must not lead to an apolitical romanticization, but should only remove from the processes of political change any basis for hatred and violence.

In the transition from a culturally more or less monocentric European church to a culturally polycentric world church, new cultural worlds are now breaking into theology itself, and political theology tries to reckon with this experience of nonidentity, this loss of ethnic and cultural innocence in our discourse about God.[16] In the discussion of inculturation, as well as in considering more generally the new point of departure in a church with diverse ethnic and cultural roots, political theology strives for a postidealist hermeneutical culture of discourse about God, and for a culture of the acknowledgment of the other as other, endeavoring to uncover the *traces of God* in the experience of the other's alterity.[17] In connection with this, it strives to replace an anthropology guided by domination with an anthropology guided by acknowledgment and acceptance.[18] Of course, if such a mentality of acknowledgment is not to end up in a vague cultural relativism, we cannot abandon the tension between the authenticity of these cultures and the universality of reason, with the human rights that are grounded therein (following what was said in section 1, above). Finally, this *Eurocentrism for the sake of the other* has also brought the theme of Europe again to the attention of political theology.[19]

In recent years I have attempted something like a theological reduction of the broader project into its individual elements. Too soon? Too forced? Not differentiated enough? Up until now, has not the whole been empirically and analytically undernourished? Is the new political theology as a consequence really anything other or more than a kind of political metaphysics? How expressive and nuanced is the word *political* here? I do not want simply to ignore these questions. However, besides the remarks which I have already directed toward these problems in chapter one of *Faith in History and Society*,[20] I would offer the following for consideration: Whenever theology wants to represent in its statements more than a postmodern religion of the psychological-aesthetic enchantment of souls, whenever it wants to offer in religion something more than a compensation for lost transcendence, yet continues to insist upon discourse about God as this has been passed on to us in the biblical tradition, it will always find itself in a precarious situation from an epistemic and epistemological perspective.[21] Given this situation, I have tried to draw attention to the category of the knowledge of absence (which is grounded in anamnestic reason).[22] This kind of knowledge has been nurtured above all in the traditions of negative theology. For me it is nurtured by the shock of which I have already spoken, the shock that comes from realizing how little in Christian discourse about God one usually hears of a history of suffering in creation that cries out to the heavens. No hint that there is something unreconciled to be found in theology! No experience of nonidentity, in which the oh-so-certain discourse about God collapses into helpless discourse with God. I know, such a negative theology runs counter to the widespread postmodernism of our hearts, with its tendency to immediate affirmation and with its provincialization of our problematic world. But without this shock, without pain over the contradictions in creation, it will be very difficult to follow the fundamental impulse of the theology presented here. It is marked by a particular sensitivity to theodicy.[23] And in all of its statements about God, God's Christ, and the world, it holds itself accountable to an eschatology which has not lost the vision of bounded time— whether that loss be due to an evolutionism fed by our scientific civilization, or an enthronement of unbounded time as the majesty of being, as in Friedrich Nietzsche.[24]

This book shall continue to be dedicated to those for whom it was originally intended. This includes, once again, Karl Rahner, that unforgettable teacher and friend, who taught me and inspired me, even in those places where I began to disagree with him theologically.

Winter, 1991/92   *Johann Baptist Metz*

2

On the Way to a Postidealist Theology

No matter how you begin, it cannot but sound somewhat pretentious when you are supposed to say what your "own" approach to theology is. Theo-logy, if it does not want to deceive itself and others, is the continual and continually renewed attempt at discourse about God, however contested and endangered it may be and however much it falls short. One could begin by trying to talk about God and, in so doing, present one's theological approach. However, one could also begin by sketching out the theological approach and then develop within it one's discourse about God. After considerable hesitation I have chosen the second option, because it is a great deal easier, and also because it better serves a comparative orientation. With this in mind, I will use the word *paradigm* interchangeably with *approach*. I use the former word, which has become quite common even outside discussions in the philosophy of science, because to me it seems well suited to describe matters of origin and unity and because, along with the term *paradigm shift*, it describes theological changes quite well.[1]

I. COMPETING APPROACHES

In looking at the Catholic Church I see three competing theological approaches at work. This is not intended to be an exhaustive description, but it does claim, all the same, to give a kind of representation by means of ideal types. I am talking about a neoscholastic paradigm, a transcendental-idealist paradigm and a postidealist paradigm. I describe the third paradigm as "postidealist" with caution, because it is only beginning to unfold—first in the attempts of the new political theology, and then, if I am right, in the theology of liberation. I understand my own theological approach as a contribution to the emergence of this postidealist theological paradigm.

I intend the distinction between the three approaches (ideal types) as an inclusive one; that is, all three are theological options in a Catholic sense. They reflect the complexity and tensions in the present ecclesial reality. Naturally, the option for one paradigm implies a theological critique of the other two.

Looking at the whole church, the *neoscholastic paradigm* is still predominant. Indeed, given recent developments in the church that reflect and, in their own way, reinforce neoconservative social tendencies, one has to speak of an Indian Summer for this paradigm. Without wishing to belittle the real service that it rendered in the nineteenth century and at the beginning of the twentieth century, this paradigm may nevertheless be characterized as above all a defensive-traditionalist, nonproductive confrontation with the challenges of so-called modernity.[2] It is telling enough that the chief work of neoscholasticism from the last century has the title "Theology of Premodernity" (*Theologie der Vorzeit*).[3] Furthermore, this striking fixation on (scholastic) premodernity corresponds to a process of intellectual and social isolation in Catholicism. Catholics gathered themselves into a mighty, and to no small degree political, *corpus catholicum*—a rather pallid imitation of the great *corpus christianum* of the Middle Ages. *Kulturkämpfe* in the social-political realm, and confrontational theology in the confessional realm, were signals of the strictly defensive way this approach worked through the challenge of modernity. Ecclesial orthodoxy appeared to be more rigorous than radical; a purely defensive rigorism began dominating the church's pastoral practices.

Thanks to what is probably the most far-reaching paradigm shift in contemporary Catholic theology, we have the *transcendental-*

idealist paradigm. It is characterized by the attempt to appropriate the heritage of the classical patristic and scholastic traditions precisely by means of a productive and aggressive dialogue with the challenges of the modern European world: the discovery of subjectivity as a crisis for classical metaphysics, and the critical-productive confrontation with Kant, German Idealism and Existentialism on one hand and with social processes of secularization and scientific civilization on the other. To the extent that the development of this paradigm is due above all to Karl Rahner, it fulfills in my view all those criteria which must be posited of a new paradigm in theology.[4] This transcendental-idealist paradigm has found its ecclesial and social equivalents in new forms of Christian and ecclesial life that, viewed in terms of the whole church, relate themselves not unjustly to the impetus of the Second Vatican Council.

Meanwhile, of course, theology has been confronted with new crises which, if they are to be grasped and dealt with in a critical and productive way, go beyond the transcendental-idealist paradigm. I am speaking here, still somewhat at a loss, of a *postidealist paradigm.*[5] I will begin by designating the new crises, and will then try to show how and in what sense the theology I am calling for here, which deals with these crises with a salvific intent,[6] is a political theology or can be named such—even though this word is not immune from misunderstandings and therefore must be explained by means of other connotations. Perhaps this paradigm has only won complete clarity, its unequivocal profile, in the contemporary struggle over liberation theology.

This new approach certainly cannot legitimate itself theologically without rendering an account of the transcendental-idealist paradigm and of the way it appropriates the classical theological traditions. That is the sense in which I have tried to pose my questions to Karl Rahner's theology. I will be taking them up again indirectly in the following attempt to stand firm theologically before these new crises—with salvific intent. In posing these critical questions regarding Karl Rahner, I do not want to deny that I owe to him the best of my own theological work, and that without him I would not even be able to ask him "my" questions.

Rahner already belongs among those classic theologians whom you continue to welcome as teachers, even when you think that you have to disagree with them.

I will present three crises that enkindled the new approach because, in my opinion, they could not be handled in either a neoscholastic or a transcendental-idealist way:

1. the Marxist challenge, or theology facing the end of its cognitive innocence and facing the end of a dualistic understanding of history;

2. the challenge of the catastrophe of Auschwitz, or theology confronted with the end of every subjectless, idealist system of meaning and identity; and

3. the challenge of the third world, or the challenge of a socially antagonistic and culturally polycentric world, theology at the end of Eurocentrism.

I will refrain from pursuing whether and to what degree one can also speak of crises confronting modernity (which occur frequently today) in terms of these three crises. For me the experience of these crises and my confrontation with them meant a certain shift in philosophical-theological background. I shifted from the transcendental Kant and from Heidegger to the Kant of the primacy of practical reason (turning once again to the theme of Enlightenment). I did that guided by the suspicion that the German philosophies upon which the transcendental paradigm was built—Idealism and Existentialism—had only overcome the Enlightenment speculatively, without really having passed through it. My critical attention was directed away from Idealism and toward the postidealist critique of religion, as well as toward the attempt by Karl Marx to conceive of the world as an historical project; it focused on Bloch and Benjamin and on the Frankfurt School's formulations of the issues. Finally, I tried to find some initial access to Jewish thought and to Judaism's long-dismissed religious wisdom. Stressing the Jewish tradition in Christianity, as distinct from the Greek-Hellenistic traditions with their ancient

tendency toward dualism, became of particular concern to me.
Besides those who were struggling with me toward a new political
theology, theological names like Kierkegaard and Bonhoeffer
became important to me, though I had no desire to distance
myself from the spirit and inspiration of my teacher. Here again,
perhaps, only the process of liberation theology has fully brought
to the fore what is intended with this new paradigm—above all in
the realm of ecclesial life.

II. THE NEW CHALLENGES—OR, ON THE WAY TO A POSTIDEALIST THEOLOGY

A. The Marxist Challenge

While it is true that the so-called Marxist challenge is well over
one hundred years old, I would still assert that it has not been
taken seriously in (Catholic) systematic theology to date. Either
we made use of the well-known theological division of labor with
which Marxism was treated in the church's social teachings, but
never effectively surfaced as a foundational problem for theology,
as a challenge to the logos of theology itself; or we practiced a
strategy in the church and in theology that I call *intellectual hibernation,* the attempt to survive challenges by freezing one's own
position so one might, after the thaw, describe the challenges as
obsolete. But the problems remain, and they haunt the dreams of
theology and the church like ghosts. I would like here to speak
very briefly of a twofold challenge posed by Marxism that reaches
right down to the logos of theology.

1. The first challenge is an epistemological one and touches
upon *the question of truth.* At issue is the relationship between
knowledge and interest. According to Marx, all knowledge is conditioned by interest. This axiom also forms the basis for ideology
critique and the critique of religion in his early works. At least
since Marx—under the subversive eyes of his ideology critique—
religion has lost its cognitive innocence, if it had not already done
so due to the Enlightenment's critique of religion and the collapse

of the religious worldviews that became manifest therein. Theology found itself to some degree in the situation of the naked emperor in the fable of the emperor's new clothes.

The first phase in the development of a postidealist theological paradigm is characterized by the attempt to reckon with this situation while continuing within it as a theology. It tried to develop an awareness that theology and the church are never simply politically innocent, and that therefore one of the fundamental tasks of systematic theology must be to take political implications into account. And this is not because the political—as Carl Schmitt would say—is the totality, but rather because suspicion of theology and of religion has become total. This postidealist political paradigm for theology starts from the fact that the processes of the Enlightenment have led neither to the complete privatization of religion nor to the complete secularization of politics. Even politically enlightened societies have their political religions through which they try to legitimate and stabilize themselves. We see this, for example, in the form of *civil religion* in the United States and as *bourgeois religion* here. Clearly, both types of political religion (which can in no way be equated, since they are from very different political cultures) serve to politicize religion, leading to its strict social functionalization. It is precisely this politicization of religion that the new paradigm criticizes, and this in two ways. First, in the fashion of a critique of religions, the new paradigm contests any religion that operates as a legitimation myth, and escapes the social critique of religions at the price of suspending its own truth-claims. Second, in a theological critique, it criticizes all theologies that, by appeal to their unpolitical character, turn into theologies of this political religion. Even if one does not want to locate the essence of religion in politics (even an enlightened politics), one may not keep silent about the political dimension of theology!

The postidealist paradigm tries to take up the challenge of Marxist ideology critique in still another way. If all empirical knowledge is determined by some interest, then not only the contents but also the subject and addressee of knowledge are significant for cognitive processes. In this sense a postidealist theology asks in a new way a question which, within the usual ecclesial division of labor, seems to be answered as if it were self-evident: the question of the subjects and the audience of the theological enterprise.[7]

Of course, in none of this has the central question arising from the first challenge of Marxism yet been formulated. It is this: How can theology take up the challenge raised by Marxist epistemology and ideology critique without thereby either surrendering or perverting the question of truth? Will not the question of truth inevitably be reduced to a question of relevance? No, it is only posed in a new form. It becomes this: Are there interests that can be qualified as being true? Interests can only be so qualified if they are universal or can be universalized: that is, if they are or can be related to all persons. For a truth is either the truth for all, or it simply does not exist. In this sense the new political theology talks about a universal or universalizable interest that is founded in the biblical traditions themselves: this is "the hunger and thirst for justice," for justice for all, for the living and the dead, for suffering past and present. The question of truth and the question of justice are related to one another: *verum et bonum convertuntur.* Interest in a strictly universal justice belongs among the premises of the search for truth. To this extent, knowledge of the truth has a practical foundation. The critical and liberating power of discourse about the truth is rooted in it.[8]

2. In my view, the epochal discovery of Marxism—speaking to begin with in a very formal way—is the discovery of the world as history, as an historical project in which human beings become subjects of their histories. In this way Marxism touches upon and reveals another central theme of Christianity: *history.* If this has not been clear enough to us in the past, now it is, because (by comparison with other great religions and cultures of our world) the specifying theme, virtually *the* fateful theme of Jewish-Christian religion, is that of history. In distinction to all the other great religions, Christianity is guided by a vision of God and history or

God in history. This becomes instantly clear if only we do not allow the Jewish heritage of Christianity to be absorbed into the Hellenistic-Greek heritage, which tends more strongly toward an ahistorical dualism. It can continue to be clear to us today unless we have already fallen victim to a growing, evolutionistically poisoned weariness with history, unless we have surrendered ourselves to the anonymous pressure of the so-called *posthistoire* in modernity.[9]

In view of the Marxist challenge, the new paradigm understands itself as a theology of history with a critical and practical intent. To begin with, it stresses that even for Christianity there is only *one* history, since talk about two histories dualistically avoids the seriousness and risk of historical life. There really is no world history with a salvation history alongside or above it. Rather, the history of salvation of which theology speaks is world history that is marked by a continually threatened and contested yet indestructible hope for universal justice: justice for the dead and for their suffering. The history of salvation is that world history in which there is hope even for past suffering.

In my view, Christian faith in a God before whom past suffering does not disappear subjectlessly into the abyss of an anonymous evolution will guarantee the unshakable standards of faith's unceasing struggle: that all persons be able to be subjects, the struggle for a universal liberation. Whenever our society's common wisdom allows itself to be guided exclusively by the fictive totality of a subjectless evolution, then not only does God become absolutely unthinkable, but in consequence the interest in universal justice vanishes as well. The latter means a justice that includes even history's victims and vanquished, to whom those of us alive and building our paradises today are still indebted, but yet whose fate cannot be touched or changed by even the most passionate struggle on the part of the living. This God is for me the only reliable foundation for that universal solidarity and justice for which human beings hunger and thirst—not only today, as it were by decree of the *Zeitgeist,* but also throughout all of human history.

This theological approach tries to acknowledge the Marxist challenge insofar as that challenge articulates the interest in a universal liberation. But in contrast to the Marxist approach, it stresses that *guilt* is not, for example, a derivative phenomenon within historical process, but an authentic one. Guilt cannot be understood as only an expression of alienation, even if theologies of guilt and of sin have operated in an alienating way. The denial of guilt is a deadly attack upon the dignity of freedom. And the acceptance of guilt before God does not prevent persons from becoming the full and responsible subjects of their histories. On the contrary: wherever guilt is denied as a primordial phenomenon, or is denounced as false consciousness, exculpation mechanisms arise in the face of the suffering and contradictions of historical life. Historical responsibility, or being a subject in history, is irrationally cut in half, and failure and catastrophe are projected one-sidedly onto the historical opponent. The question of innocence and guilt, of justice and injustice, cannot however be settled in terms of the simple political contrast between friend and foe. If and insofar as the Marxist praxis of class struggle misunderstands the motifs of interiority and denies moral guilt, at least implicitly, then it cannot count theologically as a basic principle for the historical process of liberation.[10] If and insofar as Marxist analyses of history and society are guided by this premise, they cannot be taken over unchanged by theology. This is of course true as well for all other analyses, to the extent that they are marked by purely evolutionistic theories, for even these theories are no longer innocent from a theological perspective. Because their fundamental orientation is based on the logic of evolution, they all conceive of themselves as more or less meta-theories with respect to theology. For while it is true that religion is important for them, it is only as a phase in the developmental history of a humanity that has at this point been in principle exhaustively understood and surpassed.[11] Given all these theories, theology cannot constitute or justify itself by producing a still more comprehensive pure theory. This would collapse finally into a *regressum in infinitum;* rather, it must return to the subjects of faith and their praxis.

They form the real locus of crisis, as well as of hope, and theology has in them its practical and subjectwise foundation. If, returning to the theme of guilt, the community is the locus for a guilt that has been recognized and acknowledged, then it must also prove itself to be the locus for taking on an undivided historical responsibility, a locus for the interest in universal justice and liberation. Such a theological approach will inevitably refer more strongly back to its ecclesial basis, and it will become much more energetically involved with it than the usual division of labor in the wider church would presume or than the magisterium would wish. The clearest instance of this today is the mutual interaction between liberation theology and the base community initiatives in the ecclesial life of Latin America.

B. The Challenge of Auschwitz

Christian theology is not a metaphysics indifferent to historical destiny, but rather an invocation of and witness to truth in history: "The Word has become flesh." Historical situations are immanent to the logos of theology. Sometime and somehow I (finally) became aware of the situation in which I am trying to do theology and outside of which I cannot know clearly enough where I stand theologically. For me this situation is called *after Auschwitz*. Auschwitz characterizes the crisis of the so-called modern age; but it is above all a theological crisis. In this regard it must be observed at the start that the catastrophe of Auschwitz wins its provocative character precisely because of its incommensurability. It is impossible to integrate it into History. It points theology away from the singular of History and toward the plurality of histories of suffering that cannot be ideationally explained and interpreted, but only remembered with a practical intent. Because of the way Auschwitz showed up—or did not show up—in theology, it became (slowly) clear to me how high the apathy content in theological idealism is, how incapable it is of taking on historical experiences—despite, or even because of, all its talk about history and historicity. It is clear that there is no

meaning to history that one can save with one's back turned to
Auschwitz, no truth to history that one can defend with one's
back turned to Auschwitz, and no God of history whom one can
worship with one's back turned to Auschwitz. Christian theology
must be able to perceive history in its negativity, in its catastrophic
essence, so to speak, for this is precisely what distinguishes it from
evolution. If this perception is not to turn tragic—that is, develop
into a farewell to history (what a temptation!)—then these catastrophes must be remembered with practical and political intent.
Thus we will not be led to a postidealist, political paradigm in theology by foolish actionism, nor by the transparent attempt to
duplicate in theological paraphrase politics that are already in
place or being called for elsewhere, but rather by the struggle for
history as the constitutionally endangered locus where theology
finds and witnesses to truth.

It is precisely because Christians believe in an eschatological
meaning for history that they can risk historical consciousness:
looking into the abyss. Precisely because of this, they can risk a
memory that recalls not only the successful but the ruined, not
only that which has been realized but that which has been lost, a
memory that in this way—as dangerous memory—resists identify-
ing meaning and truth with the victory of what has come into
being and continues to exist. The theology in which this memory
is articulated is no theology worked out in system concepts, but
rather a theology worked out in subject concepts, with a practical
foundation.[12] This theology continually introduces into public
consciousness the *struggle for memories,* for subject-related memorative wisdom. The subjectless system cannot be for it the locus of
truth, at least not if and insofar as it allows the catastrophic
essence of history to become present to it, an essence that must
not be allowed to disappear into a purely objective meaning or
identity-system.

This theology formulates the God-question in its oldest and
most contested form, that is, as the theodicy question. Of course,
it formulates the question not in its existentialist version, but to
some degree in its political version. This theology begins with a

question about the salvation of those who suffer unjustly, of the victims and the vanquished in our history. How could one ask about one's own salvation after Auschwitz without also asking this question? This theology continually presses for a hearing on that question in public consciousness, and tries to elucidate it as a question upon which depends the fate of human beings in their concrete existence as subjects.

> To forget and repress this question…is profoundly inhuman. For this would mean forgetting and repressing the suffering of the past, and surrendering ourselves passively to the meaninglessness of this suffering. Ultimately, no prosperity of the descendants can make up for the suffering of the ancestors, and no amount of social progress can reconcile the injustice which befell the dead. If we surrender ourselves to the meaninglessness of death, and give ourselves up to indifference toward the dead for too long, then we will be left with nothing but banal promises for the living. It is not only the growth in our economic potential that is limited, as we are being warned these days. It would seem that the potential for meaning is also limited. And this is happening as the reserves dry up, and the danger persists that the great words with which we have pressed our history onward—freedom, emancipation, justice, happiness—have in the end nothing but an exhausted, dessicated meaning.[13]

The *memoria passionis,* a profoundly biblical category, turns out to be a universal category, a category of salvation. Without this *memoria passionis,* the subject-dimension of human life becomes more and more an anthropomorphism. We have already received public notice of the successor to the human person, one which is no longer plagued by any memories of past suffering or catastrophes. *Time* magazine portrayed it on a recent cover: the robot, a quietly functioning machine, an intelligence without memories, without pathos, without morality. Is this the future of humanity? Is this the overman *[Übermensch],* the strong and pitiless one? With its *memoria passionis,* and the understandings of history and time that are operative in it,[14] Christian theology struggles against such a disappearance of the human being, against the decline of the subject and against a widespread weariness with history.[15] The theological struggle is thematized in terms of the age-old theodicy question: the question about the *justification* of God in the face of the world's history of suffering, a question which today is frequently considered obsolete or at most is asked in the secularized form of anthropodicy, and then silenced with all sorts of justificatory strategies. Of course theology, as far as I can see, cannot "solve" this theodicy question. Its task rather consists in this: to allow the question to be asked again and again, to make it clear that the question cannot be transferred to human jurisdiction, and to work out the concept of a temporally charged expectation that *God,* in God's own time, will justify himself in the face of this history of suffering. This theology conceives of the Yes to God in history as a suffering unto God that ultimately approaches even the suffering of abandonment by God that has become unforgettable to us in Jesus' cry from the cross.[16]

In contrast to some important and influential contemporary theologians, this approach certainly recognizes, as I said, a suffering *unto* God, but not a suffering *in* God, or a suffering between God and God. For, try as I may, I cannot understand how such discourse does not end up either in a duplication—however sublime—of human suffering and human powerlessness, or in a gnostic eternalization of suffering in God. Neither can I understand how such a theological explanation does not violate the horrific dignity of human suffering, that is, how it avoids infringing upon that mystery of resistance and surrender that lies beyond all theological language without, however, being itself, in the cry from the depths, speechless.

Auschwitz as a challenge. It also means this: this catastrophe should make us aware that there is a horror beyond theology, which breaks up all the familiar theological attempts at reconciliation.[17]

C. The Challenge of a Socially Divided and Culturally Polycentric World

The challenge of a socially divided and culturally polycentric world, which in my opinion compels us toward a new theological approach, is erupting more and more clearly today within the sphere of the church itself. For example, what does it mean for Catholic theology that the church no longer *has* a third-world church, but *is* more and more a third-world church with a constitutive history of origins in Europe?

It means, on the one hand, that the social conflicts in the world move to the center of ecclesial and theological awareness. Conditions that are directly contradictory to the Gospel—like oppression, exploitation and racism—become challenges for theology. They demand the formulation of the faith in categories of transformation and of a resistance that is prepared to suffer. Consequently, theology, from its own logos, becomes political.

On the other hand, a series of theological implications become apparent in this new ecclesial situation that must not be ignored in the discussion of contemporary theological approaches. The church finds itself moving from a more or less monocentric European and North American church toward a culturally polycentric global church. Symptoms and impulses in this direction already appeared at the last council. In order at least to hint at the theological significance of this transition, I would divide the prior history of the church and of theology into three epochs—in a way quite similar to Karl Rahner's suggestion. The first was a relatively brief foundational period of Jewish Christianity. The second, very long era transpired within a more or less homogenous cultural realm. This was the epoch of the development of Gentile Christianity, on Hellenistic soil and also in the closely related Western-European culture and civilization. The third epoch is that of a worldwide cultural polycentrism in the church and in theology, which is in the offing today and in which, for example, modern divisions among the churches appear primarily as a fate confined to Christianity in Europe.

In this sense theology and the church are facing the end of a more or less strict cultural monocentrism. Certainly this end means neither a collapse into an arbitrary contextual pluralism nor the enthronement of a new, non-European monocentricism within the church and in theology. The Western, European history of its origins continues to be inalienably immanent to this cultural polycentrism; what is at issue now, however, is *reciprocity* in the development of ecclesial and theological life. The new theological paradigm cannot continue to cut the ecclesial and theological situation in half. In my view this means above all two things:

First, European theology must reflect upon itself within the horizon of a *history of guilt.* Without surrendering to neurotic self-accusation, this history of guilt may not in any way be repressed. Frequently we keep it at bay by means of all sorts of subtle defense mechanisms. For example, we try to protect our ecclesial and political life from global contexts of dependency with the help of a tactical provincialism. To give another example, we have become all too practiced in the use of the category of *development*—when we speak so easily of underdeveloped peoples and cultures in the third world, or when we are happy to talk about nations in the third world as our less-developed partners, but hardly ever as our victims. Perceiving the new, culturally polycentric global church will teach us to judge our history, too, with the eyes of our victims. Against the horizon of this experience our theology must become a politically sensitive theology of conversion and repentance. Describing it as a "bourgeois religion," I have criticized that European Christianity which closes itself off from this experience.[18]

Second, theology is faced with the challenge posed by a *new beginning* in and from these poor churches of our world. The new paradigm in theology wants to highlight this charismatic shock publicly for the universal church.

First, there is a new emphasis on the one, undivided discipleship. Nourished by the discipleship of the poor, homeless and obedient Jesus, there is a political spirituality with its preferential option for the poor. When we compare Christianity to other great world religions, we see it is quite possible for it to be too pious, too mystical! The one and undivided following of Jesus always includes the mystical and the political (at least in its broader sense).[19] Certainly, "Jesus was neither a fool nor a rebel, but plainly he was equally mistaken for both. In the end he was mocked by Herod as a fool and handed over for crucifixion by his countrymen as a rebel. Whoever follows him…must be prepared to fall victim to this confusion…—ever and again."[20] A theology which does not want to indulge in irrelevant aesthetic radicalism with this sort of talk can call upon traditions of this dangerous Jesus in the history of religious orders. It can refer to the new, always mystical-political experiences of suffering that are found in the way of life that is dawning in the base communities of the poor churches, and learn from them.

For this is a *second* important impulse from these poor churches: the articulation of a new model of life for the church in the so-called Base Christian Communities, in union with the bishops and thus integrated into the apostolic succession. But also integrated into the history of testimonies to the faith, for this ecclesial initiative has been authenticated by the witness of blood of many men and women. The martyrology that can already be written for this church is literally like a crimson thread traced back from the church's present to the history of Jesus' passion. An ancient saying from our Christian tradition says: "The blood of martyrs is the seed of the church." This saying can stand as the criterion for where church and Christianity are alive in a particularly promising way today. The time of the Church pulsing with this new life will not, in my opinion, be a time of great charismatic leaders, not a time of theological masters, and not even a time of great prophets. It will be much more a time of the little ones steadfastly become subjects, a time of the little prophets, so to speak, and in this sense probably also the time of the *base*. It will not be a time of conflict between a base church and a hierarchical church, but rather of the conflict between a bourgeois religion that cannot get beyond just taking care of its members, and a messianic religion of discipleship.

Finally, there is an impulse in theology that articulates and reflects these processes and therefore struggles for a living unity between redemption and liberation. As I see it, liberation theology belongs to a postidealist approach to theology. In order to indicate the challenge that the theology of liberation presents to the whole church, I would like here to refer to what I have often called Catholicism's European dilemma. The Catholic Church has only gone along with the European history of modernity in a more or less defensive fashion. It has not really participated in the so-called modern history of freedom—particularly the processes of political Enlightenment—in a productive way, but rather for the most part has held it at arm's length. Have not Catholic ages within recent European history always been *counter*-ages: the age of Counter-Reformation, of Counter-Enlightenment, of Counter-Revolution, the ages of Restoration and Romanticism? Certainly one can here discern a great deal of sensitivity to inner contradictions and disasters in the modern history of freedom, a latent sense for its inner dialectic—that is, for the so-called dialectic of Enlightenment, with which we should have come to terms by now, at least since Auschwitz. But who would not also perceive here historical failures, failures which make it so difficult precisely for Catholics to bind together freedom and grace? In my view, if we are to overcome this Catholic dilemma in the late-modern European situation, we must get beyond the monocultural realm of the Western and European church, and so arrive at a world church that is learning how to depict and call upon the grace of God as the integral liberation of human beings, is prepared to pay the price for this historical conjugation of grace and freedom, and is prepared to take on the experience of grace and of the Spirit as an experience of resistance and of suffering.[21]

Of course it is here that the whole postidealist paradigm in theology is encountering the sharpest tensions within the church. Different visions of the future of the church in late modernity and of how it can remain faithful to the last council, visions sometimes almost diametrically opposed, are wrestling with one another. Will a vision prevail that looks backward into the pre-Reformation Western church, or a vision that tries to preserve the indispensable inheritance of the Western church precisely in connection with these new initiatives? Will a defensive or an offensive strategy for preserving tradition prevail? Will the church adopt over the long term a theology that, confronted by the challenges and crises portrayed here, will develop into a post idealist paradigm? Will we embrace the socially torn and culturally polycentric world church as an opportunity for learning, in which there are more than enough signs that Christianity, faced by great dangers, is being gripped at the roots?

III. "THE DANGEROUS CHRIST"—OR, CONCLUDING CONJECTURES ON AN INTERRUPTION OF MODERNITY

What I will try to say by way of conclusion has already been hinted at in the preceeding, but does not fit seamlessly into the outline that has been laid out. Apparently it does not fit into the contemporary theological way of doing things in general; consequently, it has for the most part been allowed to fall by the wayside. It has been theologically proscribed, repressed or even reinterpreted and rendered harmless with the help of semantic deceptions. I am talking about the *apocalyptic*. To me, the degree to which it has been repressed and forgotten appears most clearly today in the ways it is used (even by theologians and preachers) as a free-floating metaphor easily projected onto the current fears of catastrophe, onto the fear of nuclear self-annihilation. So I do not conclude with the apocalyptic because it is in this way a current issue, but because its supposed currency shows again how little we still understand about it. And I conclude by discussing it because it has exercised me over the years, because it is to a certain degree the hem of my theological approach, although I have not learned to speak consistently and convincingly about it.[22] Therefore I will call these thoughts, which have continually irritated and spurred my theology, conjectures.

1. I begin with a conjecture about the word *dangerous*, a word that became central to my thought in the formulation *dangerous memory*. In a so-called extra-canonical saying handed down to us by Origen, Jesus said, "Whoever is close to me, is close to the fire; whoever is far from me, is far from the Kingdom." I understand this saying as a condensed commentary on New Testament apocalypse. It is dangerous to be close to Jesus, it threatens to set us

afire, to consume us. And only in the face of this danger does the
vision of the Kingdom of God that has come near in him light up.
Danger is clearly a fundamental category for understanding his
life and message, and for defining Christian identity. The lightning bolt of danger lights up the whole biblical landscape, especially the New Testament scene. Danger and being in danger
permeate every New Testament statement. Thus the discipleship
stories of the synoptics are not, as everyone knows, entertaining
stories, and neither are they edifying; rather, they are stories in
the face of danger, dangerous stories. They do not invite one just
to ponder, but to follow, and only in risking this Way do they manifest their saving mystery. John confirms this also: "If the world
hates you, know that it has already hated me before
you....Remember what I have told you: the servant is not greater
than his master. If they have persecuted me, then they will also
persecute you" (15:18f.). And Paul confesses, "We are afflicted in
every way, but not crushed; perplexed, but not driven to despair;
persecuted, but not forsaken; struck down, but not destroyed" (2
Cor 4:8f.). What do we really understand about the New Testament when in our modern interpretation the presence of danger
is systematically tuned out? What, when we—zealous for enlightenment and insistent upon a strict and narrow demythologization—simply wipe away or whitewash the horizon of danger that
spans and holds together the biblical stories, especially those of
the New Testament?

What lies hidden behind our critique of apocalyptic images?
The will to become enlightened concerning the little-understood
power of the myths in these traditions? or the will to avoid the
dangerous Christ and to silence danger or, at best, to displace it
into the virtually extraterritorial situation of death? Probably
both are at work. But always also this avoidance. Indeed, there is
no dearth of attempts to interpret history *post natum Christi* as a
large-scale avoidance maneuver before the dangerous Christ. In
the course of this avoidance a Christianity arises—and I do not say
this in a denunciatory voice, but rather with a hint of mourning
and bewilderment—styled after a bourgeois, domestic religion,

one free of danger but also of consolation. For a safe and unendangered Christianity is also one that will not console. Am I deceived in this? In some regions of Christianity I see arising counterimages to a bourgeois and smug religion: for example, in those poor churches I spoke of earlier, which understand their fidelity to Christ also as liberation and seek it as liberation in the face of greatest danger. Is it presumptuous to assume that in these places a new and clearer notion is bursting forth about what it is to be close to Jesus, that is to say, what is required and promised in following the one who is supposed to have said of himself: Whoever is close to me is close to the fire?

The oft-cited saying comes from Hölderlin: Where there is danger, the salvific grows as well. Its apocalyptic converse would have to be this: Where salvation approaches, there danger grows as well.[23] The vision of salvation, as illustrated by the biblical stories, is not without its eschatological dialectic. Thus wherever Christianity becomes more at home, more easy to bear, wherever it becomes more livable and ends up for many being the symbolic exaltation of what is going on anyway and of what determines the way of the world, there its messianic future is weak. Wherever it is difficult to bear, recalcitrant and thereby promises more danger than safety, more homelessness than security, there obviously it is closer to the reality of which Jesus spoke when he said of himself: Whoever is close to me is close to the fire; whoever stands far from me, stands far from the Kingdom. Only if we recover in these onerous apocalyptic images of danger some sense of the situation of Christian hope, will the other images of hope, the images of the Kingdom of God, not collapse like images long ago unveiled as archaic daydreams. Only if we remain faithful to the images of crisis will the images of promise remain faithful to us.

2. The sickness unto death of religion is not naiveté, but banality. Religion can become banal when in its commentaries on life it only duplicates what without it—and not seldom against it—would become the modern consensus anyway. The *naiveté* of religion[24] waylays these truisms. It does this, for example, by tarrying with

the texts and images of the New Testament apocalypses a little bit longer, standing up to them for just a little bit longer than our modern consensus allows. It certainly does not want to be amicably reconciled to these texts and images with the help of a thousand subtle modifications; rather it *takes offense [ärgern]* at them. For those who originally spoke and then repeated these words were quite aware that they are indeed a stumbling block *[Ärgernis]*.[25]

With its apocalyptic images religion wants to be a stumbling block to *modernity's image of the human,* and, at least for a moment, to resist it. Its resistance is directed against that image of the person everywhere predominant today. This is the Promethean-Faustian image, wherein the person of the future is depicted without the dark background of mourning and suffering, of guilt and of death. The rebellion of apocalyptic images is directed against the image of the person devoid of mystery, incapable of mourning and incapable of allowing him- or herself to be consoled, whose living space certainly appears to have been successfully insulated from all the storms of God but who drifts ever more helplessly into the twilight of banality and into the long, drawn out death of boredom, and whose dreams of happiness end up finally being images of an unhappiness that is free from longing and suffering.

Finally, with its apocalyptic images religion wants to be a stumbling block also to *modernity's understanding of time and of history* and, at least for a moment, to resist it. This resistance, this way of interrupting what we take to be obvious, is even more difficult to grasp and can hardly be freed from the suspicion of eccentricity. It is no wonder that even theologians long ago came to terms with the modern consensus, and now see in these apocalyptic texts and images hardly anything more than the projection of archaic fears that are unbecoming in the modern person. When religion nonetheless hands down these texts and images, and suggests in them elements of a dangerous memory, it does this not in order to give a gloating commentary on the course of world history, but in order to get at the sources of our fear.

It may be that early man was always terrified by a sense of the imminent end of his life and world. Something of this also shows itself in the contemporary fear of catastrophe. But in my opinion, for the modern person there is not only the fear that everything comes to an end and that our planet is doomed to destruction; rather, there is a fear—more deeply rooted—that nothing comes to an end anymore, that there is no end at all, that everything is sucked into the swell of a faceless evolution that finally rolls over everything from behind, like the sea rolls over grains of sand, and, like death, makes everything equi-valent.

Today there is, so they say, a cult of the possible; everything is possible. Certainly, but there is also a new cult of fate: everything can be superseded. Resignation is the undertow to the sense of possibility. The two, the cult of managing our fate on the one hand and the cult of apathy on the other, belong together like two sides of a single coin. The understanding of reality that guides the scientific-technological domination of nature and draws its energy from the cult of the possible, is deeply marked by a representation of time as an empty continuum, growing evolutionarily into endlessness, in which everything is mercilessly, gracelessly enclosed. Even a planet consumed by nuclear explosion is still given up to the empty hypothermia of evolution. This understanding of time eradicates every substantive expectation, and thus engenders that secret identity-crisis that eats away at the souls of modern people. It is difficult to decipher because it is has long been practiced successfully under the ciphers of progress and development, before, in brief moments, we discover it at the roots of our souls.

The great visions break up against the sense of life that is fed by this timeless time. The great utopias flatten out more and more into intermediary strategies, as we can see happening in political life across all political blocks. What has recently been named the cynicism of modernity is also fed by this secret fear of timeless time. This is the cult of apathy, withdrawal from the danger zones of historical and political responsibility, the clever and adaptational skill of making oneself inconspicuous, of compartmentalized thinking, living life in discrete little pieces: a mentality, finally, that can turn us into voyeurs of our own dissolution. For me these are the symptoms of a widespread weariness with history in late modernity.[26]

Apocalyptic texts talk about the end of time and of history; they bring interruption into proximity. In that regard these texts and images must be scrutinized carefully. They do not contain idle speculations about the exact point in time of some catastrophe, but vivid commentaries on the catastrophic essence of time itself. In the apocalyptic's subversive vision, time itself is full of danger. Time is not just that evolutionarily stretched-out, empty and surprise-free endlessness that offers no resistance to our projections of our future.[27] Time belongs not to Prometheus or to Faust, but to God. For the apocalyptic, God is the one who has not yet fully appeared, the still outstanding mystery of time. God is seen not as that which transcends time, but as the end which is pressing in upon it, its delineation, its saving interruption. For in the view of the apocalyptic, time appears first and foremost as a time of suffering. The apocalyptic has no problem subordinating nature's time to the time of human beings' passion. For apocalypticism, a wisdom about identity announces itself in experiences of suffering, a wisdom about identity which refuses to be reduced to the trivial identity of inertia in natural temporality. For the apocalyptic, the continuity of time is not the empty continuum of evolution, but rather the trail of suffering. And respect for the dignity of the suffering that has accumulated through time impels the apocalyptic to understand nature's time from the perspective of the time of suffering and, thus, evolution from the perspective of history. This certainly does not mean ignoring the billions of years of nature's time, but rather judging it to be a sort of timeless time.

But do not all of us really feel and live this way? Who really connects the time of his or her own life with the billions of years of evolution's time? Who judges and directs his or her actions on that basis? Does this mean that we are all in the grip of a merciful illusion? Some, because they do not want to give up an eschatological hope, and others because they will not face up to their fears? Or is there a truth in apocalyptic images that has not yet been brought to light, or has been repressed? To be sure, these questions give rise in theology to the danger of being out of step with the times. If this noncontemporaneity is not to become blind or aggressive backwardness, but instead is to come into play as a creative noncontemporaneity, then the apocalyptic heritage cannot be left (as it usually is) to traditionalists or fundamentalists. What has our modern eschatology come to that it has submissively allowed apocalypticism's sting to be drawn? Has not this gentle eschatology prepared the ground for an understanding of time as timeless time? Has it not too passively adapted itself to this understanding of time? Has it not, in the name of Christ's victory, purified time of all its contradictions, and ironed it out completely? Has it not interpreted all catastrophes, all dangers and disasters only as the echoes of a receding thunderstorm? And has it not thereby contributed to the result that for us time has become a time with no destiny, an empty and surprise-free endless continuum, that therefore we have identified the semantic potential of history more or less self-evidently with the victoriousness of whatever evolution has produced? But has not the biblical God always made covenant with those who—in terms of a goal-less evolution and its power of selection—had no future, beginning with the Covenant with the weak, humble desert people of Israel, up to the alliance with the one who foundered on the cross, Jesus of Nazareth? I do not see how we can avoid the absorption of this history of God into the empty infinitude of a timeless time, unless we uncover anew the apocalyptic dimension of eschatology. In the final analysis, Christianity cannot today simply and unproblematically shift from the arena of history to that of psychology without surrendering its identity.

3

Theology as Theodicy?

I. *AFTER AUSCHWITZ*

Allow me to begin with a reference to my own theological biography. Slowly, much too slowly, I became aware—and the realization of how long I had hesitated made me even more uncomfortable!—that the situation in which I am a theologian, that is, try to talk about God, is the situation *after Auschwitz*. Auschwitz signals for me a horror that is beyond all the familiar theologies, a horror that makes every situationless talk about God show up as empty and blind. Is there, I asked myself, a God whom one can worship with back turned to Auschwitz? And can any theology worthy of the name keep on talking about God and about human beings after such a catastrophe, as if the presumed innocence of our human words would not have to be scrutinized in the face of such a catastrophe? I became uneasy: Why does one see so little (or nothing at all) of this catastrophe in theology—not to mention of humanity's histories of suffering in general? Is it possible or permissible for theological discourse to proceed at a distance in the same way as (perhaps) it is for philosophical discourse? I was disturbed by the conspicuous amount of apathy in theology, by its astonishing and obdurate befuddlement. It reminded me of an idealism which fancied that it had sublated *[aufzuheben]* the negativity of human histories of suffering into the fully grasped self-movement of absolute spirit. "After Auschwitz" signifies a fissure in my Christian and theological biography.

Since then I have asked myself whether in my theological work

I was categorically oriented too much by a subjectless and "human-empty" thinking about being, under the leveling view of which even the singularity of this catastrophe vanished. And whether, therefore, I paid too little attention to the way the Bible thinks, in terms of covenant and justice, which is to see the human person not primarily as a "neighbor to Being" but rather as a neighbor to the person, especially to the stranger who suffers. That way of thinking would urge not ontological but eschatological differences, calling them to the attention of the most progressive consciousness.

Since then my theological work has been defined by the insight that in view of Auschwitz we need to examine not only our Christian theologizing about Judaism, but also examine Christian theology—our Christian discourse about God—as a whole. In short, what is needed is the long-overdue dissolution of the clandestine marriage between Christian theology and an ahistorical Gnosticism.

As I became conscious of the situation after Auschwitz, the God-question forced itself on me in its strangest, most ancient and most controversial form, as the theodicy question; not in its existential but, to a certain degree, in its political garb: discourse about God as the cry for the salvation of others, of those who suffer unjustly, of the victims and the vanquished in our history. How could one ask about one's own salvation after Auschwitz, I realized clearly, without this question! For discourse about God is either about a vision and promise of universal justice, touching even the sufferings of the past, or it is empty and void of promise, even for those alive today. The question immanent to this discourse about God is first and foremost the question about the salvation of those who suffer unjustly. The truth that guides it is known only in committed resistance against every form of injustice that creates suffering.

In taking up once again the theme of theodicy in theology, I am not suggesting (as the word and its history might suggest) a belated and somewhat obstinate attempt to justify God in the face of evil, in the face of suffering and wickedness in the world.

What is really at stake is the question of how one is to speak about God at all in the face of the abysmal histories of suffering in the world, in "his" world. In my view that is *the* question for theology; theology must not eliminate it or overrespond to it. It is *the* eschatological question, the question before which theology does not develop its answers reconciling everything, but rather directs its questioning incessantly back toward God.

Martin Heidegger once remarked that the question is the piety of thinking. I would add: directing one's questioning back toward God is the piety of theology. The kind of theology I am trying to work out and convey here cannot solve the theodicy question. Rather, its task consists in formulating it as a question directed back at God, and working out the concept of a temporally charged expectation that, if anything, God will "justify" himself in God's own time in the face of this history of suffering. Do we believe in God? or do we believe in our beliefs in God and, in so doing, perhaps really believe only in ourselves or in what we would like to think about ourselves? Consider, however, a faith that does not believe only in itself, but really believes in God. In this world of ours, however, does not such a faith necessarily take the form of a continual questioning in a temporally charged expectation? Finally this is true even for a Christian's faith: Whoever hears the message of the resurrection of Christ in such a way that the cry of the crucified has become inaudible in it, hears not the Gospel but rather a myth. Whoever hears the message of the resurrection in such way that in it nothing more need be awaited, but only something confirmed, hears falsely. What does Paul mean, after all, when he says "if the dead are not raised, then neither has Christ been raised" (1 Cor 15:13,16)? Not even Christology is free of eschatological uneasiness. And the faith of Christians does not only sing, but cries out, as the final words of the Bible show. There is a hint of something unreconciled in Christianity. To banish this would be an expression not of faith, but of smallness of faith.

II. THE ENDURING BIBLICAL PROVOCATION

Where do all these questions and assertions lead us? They might be fine for the biblical world; however, are we not separated by a deep abyss from its ways of perceiving and thinking? Are we not worlds away from Paul? Will not the attempt to recall and press for the biblical way of talking about God in today's theology inevitably turn into a crude biblicism? Does not the attempt betray a good deal of hermeneutical naiveté? But let us see where various forms of hermeneutical naiveté are really at home! And let us be guided by the suspicion that the appeal to hermeneutics in theology can also serve to silence the provocation of the biblical discourse about God and gently disburden us of its scandal.

A typical hermeneutical disburdening strategy these days follows the so-called worldview thesis. One distinguishes between ancient (or archaic) and modern worldviews, then frankly and broad-mindedly relegates apocalypticism and theodicy, imminent expectation and parousia, along with the ways of perceiving the world that are tied to them, all together to what we like to call the mythical image of the world of archaic-biblical times. But, as I see it, this is where the real hermeneutical naiveté is hidden! Representatives of this approach act as if there were an historically and culturally naked Christianity, free of images of the world, a stripped-down biblical idea of God that one could think as easily as Plato's Ideas, and then, according to one's need, taste or skill, dress up with quite different, indeed contradictory, images of the world. But apocalypticism and theodicy, imminent expectation and parousia, as well as the perception and definition of the world that they force upon us, may not be reduced to mythical relics that have long ago been sloughed off. They are not simply at the disposal of our discourse about the God of the Bible, provided we have not long ago transformed God into a timeless Platonic Idea and refashioned Christianity into Platonism or (more clearly) into a Plotinism of the modern age, all in order to shield it from the abysses of the human histories of suffering and to spare theology the downright apocalyptic uneasiness of questioning God.

The alternative would be to attend to the enduring provocation of the biblical discourse about God: here Christology and eschatology—for the sake of parousia—are not cleanly divided, and eschatology has not had its apocalyptic sting drawn. Here Christian doctrine about the last days has not yet been changed into a gentle, evolutionary eschatology. Here the temporal tensility of hope, its character of expectation, has not yet—out of fear of being disappointed and disillusioned—been put aside or semantically turned into a timeless hope. Here bounded time is still the universal horizon of discourse about God, and the question of theodicy is still *the* eschatological question.

Would it not have to be and remain *the* question for theology today? Yet it appears the question was long ago trivialized, defused or overresponded to: by theological attempts to give meaning to the course of this world by means of universal history, for example; or by optimistic eschatologies of a salvific evolution, or by a reduction of the theodicy question to a gnosis-like myth about identity and authenticity within human existence; or by means of a suffering *in* God that is too much caught up and sublated within the Trinity rather than by means of a temporally charged suffering *unto* God; or by too many clever answers to such questions as Who is God? and Where is God? and by too little attention to the primordial biblical question, What is God waiting for? After all, the language of the New Testament closes with this question, with this cry, now christologically intensified.

III. THE AUGUSTINIAN PARADIGM

The aforementioned biblical provocation presumes that the theodicy question, questions about evil, suffering and sin in God's good creation, cannot be separated from the God question. This changed in the history of the church and of theology as a whole, beginning with Augustine. As always, the great

Augustine continues to be extremely significant even when he erred, as I think is the case here.

Augustine lived and taught in a church that, as Adolf Harnack once said, was built up against Marcion. As we all know, Marcion came out of Asia Minor during the twilight years of the early church, offering an argumentative strategy both for absorbing the disillusionment that arose from the expectation of Jesus' imminent return and for silencing the theodicy question. Against the grain of all the biblical discourse about God—that salvation has a core in time rather than a timeless core—he posited the gnostic axiom of the atemporality of redemption and the irredeemability of time, in order to discharge once and for all the tension caused by imminent expectation in the early church. Furthermore, using a gnostic dualism of a creator and redeemer God, he tried to close the open flank of the theodicy question, which accompanies the historical development of biblical discourse about God in the form of crying-out and inconsolable expectation. The early church decisively rejected his offer. It did not allow even Origen's sublime attempt to mediate it. The church did not follow him, but rather Irenaeus, the great anti-Marcionite polemicist.

In this situation Augustine set a course for theology that it has traveled for the most part even to the present day. Correspondingly, the theodicy question was increasingly marginalized in theology, and not infrequently the suspicion has been explicitly voiced that a theology that is still uneasy over this question is proceeding from a false or inadequate understanding of Christian faith.

The relevant elements of Augustine's proposal are to be drawn above all from his so-called treatise on freedom, *De Libero Arbitrio*. In this book Augustine lays the responsibility for evil and suffering in the world exclusively at the feet of humanity and its sinful history, rooted in its "no" to God. *God*, therefore, especially the creator God, is out of the picture so far as the theodicy question goes! Faced with the histories of suffering in the world, there is no eschatological questioning of God; there cannot be any, because it would lead us straight back to Marcion and his dualism between creation and redemption. The Augustinian conception is probably only intelligible as a counter-conception to Manichaeism and Gnosticism. Not God, but only a humanity-become-sinful bears the burden of responsibility for a creation that is torn and permeated by suffering. Augustine's strong doctrine of freedom really springs from an apologetic intention: an apology for the creator God. It is astonishing to see how this apology misled him into positing a human freedom that is autonomous and independent of God, the kind of freedom that has really only become familiar to us in the secularized modern age.

But can human freedom bear the burden of the histories of suffering? Can it take upon itself the responsibility for a world shot through with suffering? Is it possible or permissible to understand all the hideous suffering in the world as some sort of cosmic reflex to the sinful actions of human beings? Even Augustine is uneasy with these questions. Appealing to the Letter to the Romans, he develops the doctrine of original sin, which makes of humanity a *massa damnata,* as well as the doctrines of predestination, divine election and foreordination. Augustine continues to be unclear on these issues, indeed in a certain sense he contradicts himself. Accordingly, in my view, Augustine's theodicy paradigm contains a number of theological aporias, only the most obvious of which I will mention here.

1. It is hard to refute Hans Blumenberg's suspicion that Marcion's and Gnosticism's theological dualism between the creator God and the redeemer God has been recapitulated in Augustine as an anthropological dualism between the (few) saved in God's election and this *massa damnata,* which in the final analysis continues to bear responsibility for evil in the world, for the pollution of God's good creation.[1]

2. Augustine shares one premise with Marcion: *God* may not be drawn into this question. But this premise runs contrary to the fundamental principles of a theological understanding of freedom. Human freedom—even for Augustine and for Paul, to whom Augustine continually appeals—is not autonomous, but

theonomous; that is, it is posited, empowered and encompassed by God. Because of this, it cannot bear ultimate reponsibility for the histories of suffering in the world, and the question rebounds to some degree upon God and God's foreordained sovereignty. The oft-employed differentiation from scholastic theology between permission and causation sounds here rather like a feeble apologetic distinction. As Rahner has said:

> What does "permitting" mean, if, according to the theology of the classical schools on the relationship between divine and human freedom, there can be no doubt that God, in God's predestination, could prevent human freedom from in fact occurring as a "no" to God's holy will, without in any way infringing upon or diminishing the freedom of the creature; if, in the final analysis, it is contrary to classical theological metaphysics to assert, as a widespread vulgar apologetics does, that God must "permit" even sin in God's world if God wills, as God is quite entitled to do, that there be creaturely freedom in this world.[2]

In this context we would have to consider above all the theological understanding of paradise, of the so-called supralapsarian state of men and women. It is this understanding that includes a vision of creaturely freedom without sin, without suffering and death. From this perspective we cannot assert any indissoluble connection between creaturely freedom willed by God and the divine permission of the sin that in fact occurs in creatures. So we must say that the history of suffering raises not only a question for human guilt, but also—looking through it, as it were—a question directed back at God.

3. Discourse about God, as we know it from the biblical traditions, contains a promise: the promise of salvation, paired with the promise of a universal justice that salvifically includes even past suffering. But in Augustine "salvation" now becomes thought of exclusively in terms of "redemption," as redemption from sin and guilt. What has been lost from view is all the suffering and histories of suffering which in our everyday experience simply cannot be traced back to sin or to a history of guilt, and

which nonetheless make up the largest part of this world's suffering that cries out to the heavens. The biblical vision of salvation, the promise of salvation that is implicit in God's name *(soter)*, touches not only sin and guilt, but above all deliverance from all the situations of suffering in which men and women find themselves. In Augustine the God-question determined by the hunger and thirst for justice, that is, the eschatological question about God's justice, is replaced by the anthropocentric question about human sin. The theodicy question as *the* eschatological question is silenced.

In necessarily brief fashion I would like also to recall the *consequences* of the Augustinian paradigm for the treatment of theodicy.

1. Theology allowed no questioning of God in the face of the world's history of suffering. To a certain extent theology situated itself before an almighty and good God, and made a humanity-become-sinful alone responsible for the history of suffering. Finally and because of this it raised the impression that it was trying to reconcile itself to and collude with the almighty God behind the back, so to speak, of nameless suffering. Precisely because of this, humanity rebels against the God of the theologians; the theodicy question could, then, turn out to be the root of modern atheism.

2. The extremely exaggerated role played by the idea of guilt may be seen as an indirect consequence of this Augustinian paradigm. Echoing a famous phrase, we could label this hamartiological overburdening of humanity *the absoluteness of sin in Christianity*. It has given rise to a counterreaction that has been of far-reaching import for Christianity and theology. Freedom was exempted more and more from any suspicion of guilt; in modernity's concept of autonomy, guilt became the antipode to freedom, and the capacity for guilt had less and less validity as freedom's defining mark and as a sign of the dignity of freedom itself. Since then there have been inner-Christian, intra-ecclesial parallels to this as well. It is not by chance that the new (postmodern) enthusiasm for myths has been all the rage precisely in Christian circles. The remythicization of the Gospel message

that is on the rise today is recommended because of its dreams of innocence and its supposition that human beings are innocent—because of its ethical suspension of faith. It should be understood as a reaction to ecclesial proclamations that seem to be extremely moralistic, that are always aware only of paranetic questions about human behavior but allow no eschatological questioning of God—neither kerygmatically nor liturgically.

IV. THE ISRAELITE-BIBLICAL PARADIGM

I would like to focus once again on the situation of Christian theology after Auschwitz. Over twenty years ago I was asked during a formal discussion (echoing a famous saying of Theodor Adorno) whether there can still be prayer for us Christians after Auschwitz. Finally, I gave the answer that I would still give today: "We can pray *after* Auschwitz because there was prayer even *in* Auschwitz." Expressed in different terms, this means that we Christians can no longer get back before Auschwitz; we cannot get beyond it alone, but only together with the victims of Auschwitz. This became for me the basis of Jewish-Christian ecumenism, an ecumenism which also has consequences for Christian theology and its treatment of the theodicy question. I will give three aspects of what I would call an Israelite-biblical paradigm in connection with this question, a paradigm that in my opinion has been too long absent from Christianity. These three aspects point to repressed or forgotten elements in Christian theology; with that in mind, what follows has primarily the character of a corrective to the prevailing theological approaches, a corrective of which Søren Kierkegaard once said: "Now whoever shall present a 'corrective' must study the weak sides of what exists carefully and fundamentally—and then bring the contrary one-sidedly into play: thoroughly one-sidedly."[3] I admit that this kind of "one-sidedness" also permeates the following considerations. Their purpose is to force the contemporary theological treatment of the theodicy question back upon certain fundamental characteristics of the biblical experience of God and of discourse about God.

1. A fundamental weakness of Christian theology when confronted by the theodicy question is, in my view, rooted in a concealment of theology's spirit that occurred very early. Did not Christian theology cut itself in half in a dangerous way very early on by taking its faith, to be sure, from biblical traditions, while taking its spirit *[Geist]* exclusively from late-Greek thought regarding being and identity, from an ahistorical and subjectless metaphysics of ideas and of nature? As Joseph Ratzinger just recently formulated it, "Christianity is the synthesis that is mediated in Jesus Christ between the faith of Israel and the Greek spirit."[4]

Without wanting to deny the importance of the Greek spirit for Christianity, the question still remains: Had Israel then no spirit to offer to Christianity? Are we to understand Pascal's famous distinction between the God of the philosophers and the God of Abraham, Isaac and Jacob to mean that in the Abrahamic traditions God is not thought, but "only" believed in? Is there then in the New Testament something for thought only in those places (in the Pauline and Johannine writings, for example) where it has already been influenced by the late-Greek spirit? No, the Israelite-biblical traditions offer Christian theology something original for thought and for the spirit *[Geist]*. What is at issue here—something that has been obstinately concealed in traditional Christian theology—is thought as memory, as historical remembrancing *[geschichtliches Eingedenken]*.[5] What I am talking about here is the fundamental anamnestic structure of mind and spirit that cannot be identified with Platonic anamnesis, lifted out of time and history. In this sense it would have to be maintained that Israel belongs not only in the history of faith, but also in the history of Christianity's spirit, and of its theology.

Two sorts of forgetfulness correspond to this remembrancing: not only that which wipes away every trace so that finally nothing more can be recalled, but also that sort of forgetfulness that we think of as successful remembering: remembering through historicism, through scientific objectification and explanation of what has occurred in the past. Even this remembering remains a form of forgetting in which we separate the past from us and make it into something foreign in order to be able to depict and explain it. All historicism, consequently, is also a sort of forgetfulness. But remembrancing calls to mind the forgetfulness that is hidden in every successful objectification, a forgetfulness that marks the subversion of remembrance within an evolutionistically tinged modernity, for which what has disappeared is *ipso facto* irrelevant and whatever cannot be brought back is in every case insignificant. Remembrance, which is always on the trail of the forgotten—which, analogously to the Old Testament proscription of images, aims at a culture sensitive to absence—would really be the organ of a theology which, as theodicy, tries to confront our most progressive consciousness with what has been forgotten in it: the grievances and complaints of the past.

Is it not this kind of remembrancing that is lacking, and right in the heart of contemporary Christianity here in the middle of Europe? The recent so-called conflict among historians over the assessment of Auschwitz continually raised for me this thought: Perhaps the reason our dealings with the catastrophe of Auschwitz are so uncertain and divisive is that we lack the spirit which was to have been once and for all extinguished there. We lack the anamnestic spirit that would be necessary to perceive what has happened in such a catastrophe as well to us, to Europe, and ultimately to our discourse about God.

2. Christian theology is discourse about that God whom we—with Paul, with the New Testament—confess as the God of Christians and Jews. Precisely as a Christian theologian after Auschwitz, I have always asked myself this question: What is it finally that makes Israel—following Paul's insight—indispensable, even for Christianity? How do we recognize the finger of God in this people, to use a biblical metaphor? What is it that distinguished pre-Christian Israel, what is it that distinguished this small, culturally rather insignificant and politically humble desert folk from the glittering high cultures of its time? In my view it was a particular sort of defenselessness, of poverty, in a certain sense Israel's incapacity successfully to distance itself from the contradictions, the terrors and chasms in its life—by, for

example, mythicizing or idealizing the context in which it lived. Israel knew no mythical or ideational riches of spirit with which it could rise above its fears, the alienation of exile, and the history of suffering that was always breaking out in its midst. In its innermost essence, it remained mythically and ideally mute. It showed little talent for forgetting, and at the same time little talent for spontaneous idealistic ways of dealing with disillusionment and disappointment. Even when it imported a store of myths and idealizing concepts and mimicked them, it was still never completely consoled by them. One could almost say then that Israel's election, its capacity for God, showed itself in this particular form of its poverty and incapacity: the inability to let itself be consoled by myths and ideas. This is precisely what I would call Israel's poverty of spirit, in which it was mindful of itself in the remembrance of God.

Israel's fidelity to God expressed itself in this form of poverty. In the final analysis, Israel remained always (to use a saying of Nelly Sachs[6]) a "landscape of cries": its faith did not so much lead to answers for the suffering it experienced; rather it expressed itself above all as a questioning arising out of suffering, as an incessant turning of its questions back to—Yahweh. We need to take this form of poverty of spirit seriously if we would not fall back into the aporias of Augustine and his "response" to the theme of theodicy. As we know, Jesus himself praised poverty of spirit as blessed.

3. Poverty of spirit is the foundation of any biblical discourse on God. It also separates biblically-inspired mysticism from that mythos which, for its part, knows only answers, but no disturbing questions. If we are to get to the roots of theology as "theodicy," then this mysticism has to be discussed.

I will describe it tentatively here as a mysticism of suffering unto God. It is found particularly in Israel's prayer traditions: in the Psalms, in Job, in Lamentations, and last but not least in many passages in the prophetic books. This language of prayer is itself a language of suffering, a language of crisis, a language of affliction and of radical danger, a language of complaint and grievance, a language of crying out and, literally, of the grumbling of the children of Israel. The language of this God-mysticism is not first and foremost one of consoling answers for the suffering one is experiencing, but rather much more a language of passionate questions from the midst of suffering, questions turned toward God, full of highly charged expectation. These mystics are no willing yes-men, neither assertive nor apathetic. They practice neither cowardly submission nor masochistic self-subjugation. They are not pious underlings. Their yes to God does not express shallow humility or infantile regression. And the prayer that expresses their yes is not a language of exaggerated affirmation, no artificial song of jubilation that would be isolated from every language of suffering and crisis and which all too quickly falls suspect to being a desperately feigned naiveté. What occurs in this language is not the repression but rather the acceptance of fear, mourning and pain; it is deeply rooted in the figure of night, in the experience of the soul's demise. It is less a song of the soul, more a loud crying out from the depths—and not a vague, undirected wailing, but a focused crying-out-to.

Jesus' God-mysticism is also a part of this tradition. His is in an exemplary way a mysticism of suffering unto God. His cry from the cross is the cry of one forsaken by God, who for his part had never forsaken God. It is this that points inexorably into Jesus' God-mysticism: he holds firmly to the Godhead. In the God-forsakenness of the cross, he affirms a God who is still other and different from the echo of our wishes, however ardent; who is ever more and other than the answers to our questions, even the strongest and most fervent—as with Job, and finally with Jesus himself. "And why do you pray to God when you know that no one can understand his answers?" asked the young Elie Wiesel of the sexton of Sighet. And he answered, " So that he might give me the power to ask the right questions."[7] This counsel, which would have us repeat our cries and calling-out as a question—in our terms, as an incessant eschatological turning of our questions back unto God—points in my opinion toward a God-mysticism that is rooted in Israel and that we can in no way dismiss as too negative. It is found today, finally, wherever we pose to ourselves the ultimate and decisive God-question, the question about God in the face of the world's abysmal history of suffering.

But is such mysticism at all consoling? Does not the biblical God want above all to be consolation for those who have collasped in suffering, reassurance for those who are driven by the anxiety of existence? Here in my opinion everything depends on not misunderstanding the biblical promises of consolation. Our secularized modernity has been able neither to respond to nor to eliminate the longing for consolation. Accordingly, today we are offered—in a quasi-postmodern way—myths and fables for their potential to console. And Christianity is obviously deeply receptive to this offer. In this we can see how confused we have allowed ourselves and others to become about the biblical meaning of consolation.

Was Israel, for example, happy with its God? Was Jesus happy with his Father? Does religion make one happy? Does it make one mature? Does it give one identity? home, security, peace with oneself? Does it soothe anxieties? Does it answer questions? Does it fulfill our wishes, at least the most ardent? I do not think so.

Then why religion? What are its prayers for? To ask God for God, is finally what Jesus has to say to his disciples about prayer (Lk 11:1–13, esp. vv. 11, 13). Strictly speaking, he has promised no other consolation. At any rate, biblical consolation does not remove us to a mythical realm of tensionless harmony and questionless reconciliation with ourselves. The Gospel is no catalyst or automated assembly line for human self-discovery. In my opinion, this is where all the critics of religion from Feuerbach to Freud have been mistaken. Poverty of spirit, the root of all consolation, is not without a mystical uneasiness of questioning, not even in Christianity. Even Christian mysticism is to be understood as a mysticism of suffering unto God. From a book of Eugen Biser's I will take the story that Walter Dirks told of his visit to a Romano Guardini already marked by death:

> No one who had been there would have ever been able to forget what the old man confided on his death bed. At the last judgment

he would not only allow questions, but would also himself ask questions; in great confidence he hoped that the angel would not refuse him the true answer which no book, not even the Scriptures themselves, no dogma and no teaching office, no "theodicy" and theology, not even his own, had been able to give him: Why, God, the dreadful detour on the way to Heaven, the suffering of the innocent, why sin?[8]

The mystical uneasiness of questioning, as it has been expressed here, does not correspond, for example, to a typically intellectual cult of questioning, which indeed would be precisely the most distant from those who actually suffer. Not vaguely undirected questions, but surely passionate and focused questioning belongs to that mysticism in which we have to form ourselves in order to find true consolation. And this above all if we do not forget that biblical-Christian mysticism is not really a mysticism of closed eyes, but an open-eyed mysticism that obligates us to perceive more acutely the suffering of others.

V. SUFFERING UNTO GOD OR SUFFERING IN GOD?

Is there perhaps too much negative theology in my explanation of the theodicy theme? Where is there anything of the wealth of material offered by contemporary theology that interprets the human history of suffering using themes from trinitarian theology? Does it not belong to the specifically Christian treatment of the theodicy question to see suffering sublated [aufgehoben] in God Godself? Have not the suffering God, suffering between God and God, and suffering in God all been discussed with great seriousness and theological thoroughness—from Karl Barth to Eberhard Jüngel, from Dietrich Bonhoeffer to Jürgen Moltmann, and in the realm of Catholic theology, above all, by Urs von Balthasar? Certainly. Nevertheless, I cannot follow this approach. What I see in these worthy attempts is *too much* of a response, soothing the eschatological questioning of God. Is there not in them still too much of a speculative, almost gnostic reconciliation with God behind the back of the human history of suffering? And do not these ways of responding underestimate the negative mystery of human suffering that will not allow itself to be harmonized under any other name?

I will explain my hesitation. How is the discourse about a suffering God in the end anything more than a sublime duplication of human suffering and human powerlessness? How does the discourse about suffering in God or about suffering between God and God not lead to an eternalization of suffering? Do not God and humanity end up subsumed under a quasimystical universalization of suffering that finally cuts off the counterimpulse resisting injustice? Or is there not perhaps too much Hegel at work here, that is, too much reduction of suffering to its concept? Finally, I have always wondered whether or not there is in this discourse about a suffering God something like a secret aestheticization of suffering at work. A suffering which makes us scream or finally leaves us wretchedly silent knows no majesty; it is nothing exalted, nothing noble. This kind of suffering is completely different from a sturdy, solidaristic sharing of suffering. It is not so much a sign of love, but rather much more a frightening symptom of no longer being able to love. It is a suffering that leads to nothingness, if it is not a suffering unto God.

I do not think Christology necessitates or even legitimates our speaking of a suffering God or of suffering in God. But is it not absolutely necessary to speak of it for another reason? Must we not speak of it if we want to deflect the suspicion of apathy from a creator God in the face of conditions in his creation that cry out to heaven? Do we not read in 1 John, "God is love"? How could we do justice to this biblical statement, if we did not speak of a suffering God who suffers *with* this creation of his that is shot through with suffering? Here, in conclusion, I come back to a remark I made at the outset. If one does not begin with a Greek or neo-Pagan way of thinking about being, but rather proceeds from that biblical thinking—in terms of covenant and justice—in which every statement about being has a temporal mark ("I will be who I will be"), then one must also hear the Johannine statement "God is love" as a statement bearing the character of a promise: God will prove Godself to us as love. With Hans Jonas, who has given us much of worth to reflect on concerning the "concept of God after Auschwitz,"[9] I would like to stress that God must not be thought of as a timeless beyond; but neither—and here probably in disagreement with Jonas—may God be thought of as a dramatic "product" of an unending evolutionary time. Rather God must be thought of as the one to whom time belongs, as the end that sets its bounds.[10] To be sure, if God's creative power is thought of as an omnipotence removed from time, as an omnipotence in timeless repose, so to speak, and if this power is then confronted after the fact with creation's history of suffering, then it collapses into irredeemable contradictions. As I see it, however, this is not the case if the creative power is thought of as a power setting bounds, as the end of time coming toward it, in which alone it will be proven what it "is" and how it sustains us.

Of course, such an attempt (a quite stammering one) to do justice to the idea of God's creative power in the face of a catastrophe like that of Auschwitz has its price. I could formulate it once again in this way: Even Christian theology, drawing on its doctrine of creation, cannot eliminate the apocalyptic cry, "What is God waiting for?" Not even Christian theology can allow Job's question to God, "How long yet?" to fall silent in a soothing answer. Even Christian hope remains accountable to an apocalyptic conscience. Hans Jonas wanted to give to the victims of Auschwitz "something like an answer to their cries to a mute God which faded away so long ago." Christians are only engaging in Christology after Auschwitz when they do not make inaudible to their Christianity those "cries that faded away so long ago." Only then are they reading the horrifying record of our history with the eyes of faith, without sneaking past the epicenter of the earthquake in faith's history. In this sense theology is, and will continue to be, theodicy.

4

Theology versus Polymythicism:
A Short Apology
for Biblical Monotheism

I

In presenting this brief apology I must work under a presupposition for which I probably cannot presume universal agreement: that theology can be considered cognitively respectable and a worthy subject of philosophical discussion not only when it proceeds as historiography or ideology-critique with itself as object, but even when it tries to do nothing but defend itself.

To make it possible to discuss the confrontation between theology and the new mythology, I will avail myself of a mediation that may seem unwieldy or even misleading: the question about time. As we all know, one of the great philosophical works of this century pressed for the recognition of the importance of this question, even if it hardly resolved it. Furthermore, it is a question that has eked out a marginal, at best subordinate existence in contemporary theology. By means of this mediation the problem resolves itself in a way that might strike us as surprising. I would like here at the beginning to present openly to you this way of formulating the issue. There is a master myth that does not seem to be in need of or capable of justification, but is operative as a mythical totality in the background of modernity. It is under its anonymous pressure that we think and act "rationally." It is a myth about time, a myth that imagines the world against an unbounded temporal horizon, a horizon that has been evolutionistically unbound. The tacit interest of the reigning rationality is the fiction of time as an empty infinitude, free of all surprise, which could perhaps become de-energized,[1] but never ends and mercilessly, gracelessly *[gnadenlos]* encloses everything, annihilating every substantive expectation. The dominion of this myth of time culminates in the death of history, and of the human person, as we have trusted in him and entrusted ourselves to him in the course of history. This dominion is not broken by the still- or postmodern polymythicism, but rather is powerlessly and uncritically mirrored. In this situation the theologian urges another look at the Jewish-Christian idea of God, and the imaginative perception of the world corresponding to it, within the horizon of bounded time. From a theologian's perspective this would save the substance of historical life and, as well, a human freedom that is proper to a subject and not just arbitrary spontaneity.

Such is the central idea for my little apology for the Jewish-Christian way of thinking about God, in contrast to the polymythicism that is again burgeoning in our midst today. I am quite aware that the latter, for its part, has a suspicion of unprecedented sharpness concerning the Jewish-Christian idea of God, particularly in its monotheistic form. Frequently this idea, secularized and ideologized, is held to be the truly dangerous mono-myth that stands in the background of modernity: as godfather of a predemocratic way of thinking centered on a sovereignty that is hostile to any notion of separation of powers, and father of an obsolete patriarchalism. It is viewed as the wellspring or vanguard of totalitarian ideologies of history, a conceptual shorthand for a master narrative that endangers individuals, the expression of a thinking-from-principles that violently absorbs all diversity and all the complexly intertwined diversity and multiplicity of life and its stories. In this view, this way of thinking does not only think about something, but rather, in its dogmatic rage for consistency, thinks everything to its end,

thinks from the beginning to the end, and does not in so doing
shy away from terroristic consequences.[2]

Only a blind apologetics could assert that these and similar sus-
picions have no relevance at all for theology and its secularized cor-
relates. But do they touch the saving core? And (so the apologete in
me asks) what do they offer in the face of the dangers we all feel,
even though we interpret them in diverse ways? I, at any rate, cannot see any theological-political perspective in the neopolytheistic
and myth-enraptured atmosphere of our still- or postmodern
world; rather, all I can see ultimately is that the substance of Jewish-
Christian religion is rendered problematic, and that we are threatened with the atrophy of our political culture. I do not trust the
promise of relief from the burdens of decision, and the promise of
liberation to become individuals, that are bound up with the dis-
missal of unity-thinking and the aesthetically-mythically structured
ascent to diversity-thinking. Is not a new violence hidden precisely
in this world of unrelational and actionless multiplicity? Have we
not in our own nation lived through a dangerous suspension of the
idea of the unity and equality of all persons? Were not the Jews,
before they were sent to the gas chambers, metaphysically and
legally excluded from this unity? Can we afford, politically and culturally, to propagate that innocence which we advocate aesthetically
with our praise of polymythicism? And can we afford to forget the
horrors of mythically spellbound, polytheistic worlds? What does
the propagation of a new paganism really come down to—with its
Nietzschian rhetoric in France, and with a rather more bourgeois-
tempered (hence more deceptive) rhetoric among us? Does it not
really come down to our thinking once again (however sublimely
this time around) that the progressive forgetfulness of the horrors
of our past is a progress that saves us?

II

As a first step in my short apology allow me to sketch out why,
as already mentioned, I would shift the suspicion of totality onto
the myth of time. It is the myth of an evolutionistically

unbounded time, under the pressure of which we think and act and imagine the rational universe.

A representation of time as an empty continuum, extending evolutionarily into endlessness, dominates modernity's background. Such a representation has not only made God unthinkable and brought forth the affectively flat God-lessness of our late modernity, it has also progressively dissolved the substance of a tradition of thought in which we name historical time and the hermeneutic that is appropriate for it. Nothing which was can finally be saved from its graceless equi-valence. The historical *[historische]* relationship to the past that stands under the tacit pressure of this myth of time "presupposes not only that this past is past; it clearly also functions to overcome what once was and to ensure its irrelevance. History *[Historie]* has replaced tradition, and that means it occupies its place."[3] Under the anonymous pressure of this myth of time, memory and narrative lose their cognitive force, their substantiality; with the new polymythicism, they turn into compensatory categories.

In my view it is this time-myth that has driven the processes of the European Enlightenment into those contradictions spoken of by the "Dialectic of Enlightenment." Of course this calls for a more detailed demonstration, which I cannot provide here. Allow me, the theologian, to ask in a perhaps seemingly flippant way the following question: Was it not already the modern background-myth of time that pushed Kant into a transcendental idealization of the concept of time? And did it not force the antitranscendental Marxism to think about its revolutionary project of history *[Geschichte]* in a strictly evolutionary way, so that Walter Benjamin, surely provoked in this case by Jewish traditions, gave the well-known counterrepresentation to the Marxian image of revolutions as the locomotive of worldhistory: "Perhaps things are completely different. Perhaps revolutions are the human race, traveling on this train, reaching for the emergency brake."[4]? And is not contemporary philosophy today taking flight from nature and history into a sort of anthropological reduction of the experience of time, in order to save, with a mythically and narratively enthused "inconsistent" and "antiprincipial" compensatory mode of thought, the multiplicity, variety and individuality of the life-world that was long ago mercilessly corroded away by the myth of unbounded time? But how can thinking hope to save through compensation something that, as reasoning that perceives, plots and organizes, it long ago surrendered to this myth of time?[5]

It is clear to me that contemporary theology is also under the spell of this modern myth of time, and this is basically connected with what I call the gnostic wound of theology's logos, on which I will try to elaborate later. Because theology early abandoned the concept of time immanent to its own logos, it has become defenseless against, even receptive to, the mythical totality that lurks in modernity's background. Long before philosophy, theology excluded memory and narrative—which are indispensable for the presentation of its understanding of time and history—from its logos, degrading them to the level of categories of compensation or decoration.[6] Nowhere has the anthropological reduction of world, time, history and society been carried through as consistently as in the mainstream of modern theology.[7] Where it has not been turned into a mere theology of death by means of anthropological reduction, its eschatology is for the most part evolutionistically tinged.[8] It is not because its own logos continually forces it back into mythology that theology is mythological, but rather because theology has surrendered itself to the mythical totality standing in modernity's background.

As I see it, the dominance of this myth is making its presence felt ever more clearly in our political-cultural life as well. In my view it is not revolutionary euphoria, but evolutionistic apathy that characterizes public life at the end of this century. The looming threat I see for our political culture is not overpoliticization, not too much undetached praxis, but much more a sort of profound apoliticality, a privatistic parochial thinking always ready to adapt itself, a rather voyeuristic way of dealing with social and political crises. I would like to ask Odo Marquard this: Is it really a revolutionarily sharpened attitude of imminent expectation that threatens our political life?[9] Or is it not much more an evolutionistically relaxed resignation, overwhelmed by the experience of an empty, in some ways timeless time? This is a resignation which long ago penetrated to the spiritual foundations of our social life, even before we were supposed to become successfully practiced in it under the rubrics of these new myths. Is it not our culture industry, the growing power of the mass media (not least, of television), which as time goes on quasitranscendentally overarches everyday life and in various entertaining ways relieves us more and more of ourselves, of our own memory, our own perceptions and our own language, turning us finally into voyeurs of our own history? Does not this culture industry go out of its way to promote a pacified subjectivity, a suspension of action and distance from decision? Furthermore, does it not above all strive to bring about a farewell to history? It is not just being condemned to praxis that can take on features of terrorism, but also being condemned to the suspension of praxis. To be sure, nobody dies terrible deaths anymore from such a gentle terrorism: people are already dead anyway, before they die.

In conclusion, is it actually History *[die Geschichte]* that threatens us politically and culturally, or is it not really the polymythic world of post-history? For when history is brought to a standstill by the anonymous pressure of an evolutionistically unbounded time, what really follows is that "politics passes over into administration, every possible event is treated as a case, or only those events are allowed that can be registered as an 'instance'; individual decision is renounced or reduced to possible variations of (quasi-) ritual actions. This leads to the dissolution of individual historical persons into specimens of readily calculable universals."[10] Does not the standstill of history hurl the individual into the giddy sense of an acceleration of evolutionistically unbounded time "in which there are fewer and fewer 'stops' in the present,"[11] with an extremely high turnover in consumption and in fashions, even cultural fashions? Might it not be that a new polymythicism would contribute to the loss of imaginative capacities for perception and resistance that is showing up in all this? Are we to address the problem by literalizing our history (in a postmodern fashion), by turning it into a citation, a collage, an object of diversion? Can we really afford such innocence in our dealings with history? Are not ethical suspension and the presumption of innocence for human beings within the new myths unveiled here as an exculpation strategy, as perhaps the most sublime form of late modern anthropodicy? The argument goes something like this: faced by the catastrophes that have accumulated in their history, the only absolution human beings can find is that there simply *are no* humans-as-subjects to which guilt can be attributed.

III

I want now to come more to the point, to talk about Nietzsche. Without a doubt he is the father of the new mythologies (even if he is disavowed with some embarrassment from time to time), and he instructs us with the greatest precision on what is at stake. He knew and named the premises of the new mythological thinking. The first premise is this: God is dead. Nietzsche inscribed God's obituary into the hearts of Western civilization. But Nietzsche also spoke of a second premise that follows inexorably from the first: the person is dead. Nietzsche also wrote the obituary for the human person, the one on whom we have relied and to whom we have entrusted ourselves in our history up until now. He spoke of the death of the subject; he held the subject to be a mere fiction, and talk about the *I* to be anthropomorphism.[12] He described the distintegration of the cognitively competent subject in the subjectless, giddy play of metaphors.[13] He announced the end of historical time, since once the horizon of God is erased history collapses into an anonymous, temporally unbounded evolution that wills and seeks nothing except evolution.[14]

Nietzsche ripped the disguise from the mythical totality standing in modernity's background. He forced modernity to own up to its consequences, which he formulated as the premises of his own teachings on myths: the death of God, the death of the person. That which we innocently and naively still call the person has been an anachronism for a long time; that person, if there was supposed to be such a thing once, really does not exist anymore. Any adequate grasp of our present situation must begin with that person's death. At least for French thinkers, this death of the person is a done deed after Nietzsche. And German thoroughness has already explained it and integrated it within a theoretical system: there are no subjects, only self-referential systems. In these systems it is not the spontaneity of historical freedom that rules (quaint and archaic European notion!), but rather the intergalactic cold of an endlessly indifferent evolution. The only thing in it that reminds us of the persons we once were is at best a formless anxiety that has little to do with truth or action. This is not Nietzsche, admittedly, but someone who is rather skeptical concerning myths: Niklas Luhmann.[15]

But can even Nietzsche himself escape the spell of this image of time and of the person he has seen through? His own well-known counterproposal was also formulated as a proposal about time: the doctrine of the eternal return of the same. He called this his "most profound idea."[16] The doctrine of the return of the same (to which above all Martin Heidegger's extremely suggestive reflections have returned again and again[17]) is very closely connected to the doctrine of the overman *[Übermensch]*. The two belong together like the two sides of a coin. Nietzsche mistrusted any merely compensatory anthropology. As he sees it (correctly, I think), anthropology has lost once and for all to that against which it fights. It can never make good to the person what it long ago surrendered because of its resignation before the ruling myth of time. Nietzsche is not interested in compensation, but in the substantive reversal of the process of modernity. The character of being should be marked by boundless becoming, the highest expression of the will to power, as he called it in a note from 1885 designated as a "recapitulation."[18] Passing away should be represented as a constant becoming within the eternal return of the same, and be constantly and lastingly effected so as to overcome the will's aversion to time.

Here I would suggest that even Nietzsche's radical mythology is still a victim of that time-myth which it tried so perceptively to contest. This suggestion might very well shed light on the fate of the idea of the overman. By now we have had some historical experience of how Nietzsche's idea of the overman plays itself out, effectively preventing us from treating him without a sense of horror. What I find most frightful is the fact that the most trivial actualization of the overman could very well be the most probable one. Some years ago *Time* magazine already portrayed as its Man of the Year the one who followed the death of the person, the successor to the person: the robot. It is a computerized intelligence that no longer suffers from any passing away, no longer suffers the will's aversion to time, since it cannot forget anything. It is an intelligence without history, without pathos and without morals, a rhapsody of innocence congealed into a machine. In this way the overman, with its will to recast boundless becoming into permanence, could end up being the very apotheosis of the mythical totality it was once and for all intended to smash. I must leave off here, with that suggestion.

Something else in Nietzsche interests the apologist in me, something that can lead back through him to the thesis with which I began. It has to do with the clairvoyant connection he made between the death of God and the death of the person. Nietzsche knew that the echo to the cry of his wild man, "Where is God?" is "Then where is man?" I would conclude from this a converse, which I will try to illuminate in the following discussion: whoever would resist the vanishing of persons and their historical world, whoever would save their identities as subjects, their language that seeks truth, their ability to come to understand one another, their unsated hunger and thirst for justice, whoever wants to do these things will find it less and less possible without adopting a theological horizon. What our modern or postmodern time, already mythically committed to the death of the person and history, needs to address is the subversion of the idea of God preserved in the Judaeo-Christian traditions, which perceives and establishes the world against a horizon of bounded time. That idea will both require and enable us to keep on speaking about humanity and solidarity, about oppression and liberation, and to protest against injustice that cries out to heaven.[19] This is why it is not polymythicism but theology that would provide a defense of the person. And the new mythology, along with its polymythicism, would turn out to be something like the religion and worldview that comes after the death of history and the death of the person.

I am well aware that every apology quickly falls victim to the suspicion of being thoughtless demagoguery or sophistry. Probably this will, also. With that in view, I shall try to shed some light on the Christian discourse about God that I have so often invoked for the purpose of breaking the mythos of modernity. In so doing I shall try to save it from the suspicion with which the contemporary discourse of polymythicism attacks it.

IV

I will begin by looking at pre-Christian Israel. This small, culturally and politically rather insignificant desert people was distinguished from the glittering high cultures of its time by the painful way it was involved with reality, by its profound thissidedness, or inability successfully to distance itself from the horror of reality by means of idealizing it, mythologizing it, or by compensatory thinking. In his *Theology of the Old Testament,* Gerhard von Rad has stressed (correctly, in my view) "that Israel perceived the suffering and dangers in its life in a highly realistic fashion, that it saw itself defenselessly and vulnerably exposed to them, and that it showed little talent for taking refuge from them in any sort of ideology....Rather, it possessed an uncommon power to stand its ground before negative realities, to acknowledge and not repress them even when they could not be coped with spiritually or intellectually.[20]

Repeatedly conquered and infiltrated by foreign cultures, Israel certainly imported and mimicked its share of myths and idealization strategies from various places (Persia, Egypt, and later Hellenism). But it was not soothed or consoled by them. Israel is the people that is unable to let itself be consoled by myths. As I see it, this is why Israel can never be left behind, even for Christianity. This is what distinguishes Israel's poverty of spirit, which is the presupposition and the price for its idea of God. Israel is always a "landscape of cries," including Job's cry of complaint, "How long?"[21] and Jesus' cry of abandonment from the cross. Israel's faith does not end up as simply consoling and distancing answers to suffering; rather, it is always a disconsolate questioning from out of the midst of suffering, an incessant questioning of Yahweh. But how is this crying out to Yahweh not once again the product of an idealization? How is it still not just "the mythological encipherment of that which is eternally outstanding in a future that human beings create out of their own emptiness, only (finally) to let it retreat to that nothingness from which it arose?"[22] What does it mean that Israel has faith in Yahweh—and not just faith in its faith in Yahweh, which would really just be faith in itself and in the Yahweh-myth it produces in order to deal with disappointment and suffering?

The Israel that is this-sidedly gifted and involved in the world has not, according to all the important witnesses, experienced and thought its saving God outside the world, as transcending time, but rather as time's end, coming toward it and bounding it.[23] Such is the experience of God found in the Abrahamic traditions: "God draws Abraham onto the path." It is true of the text from Exodus, "I will be with you the one I will be with you"; it is true of the message of crisis and conversion in the prophets, in which the landscape of Israel is transformed into an eschatological landscape; finally, it is true of late Jewish apocalyptic and its theodicy, which so deeply permeates the New Testament. God "is" in coming.[24] This coming, which can be neither extrapolated nor anticipated, constitutes "the primal stratum of the imaginative perception of reality" in late Jewish and New Testament thought.[25] At its beginnings this apocalypticism is certainly not—as its critical investigators like to presume[26]—an ahistorical, catastrophe-driven speculation concerning the point in time at which the world will end. Rather it is the—to be sure, categorically distorted—attempt to uncover the bounded essence of the world's time itself, from which, in the final analysis, the historical time of an individual's life cannot and must not be decoupled. What is at issue here is not just an historical time contained in a cosmos transcending that time, but the temporalization of the cosmos itself within the horizon of bounded time.[27] Here, at this crossroad between pre-Christian Judaism and Christianity, the proper element of the biblical idea of God becomes evident, the element which separates it from Middle Eastern and Persian dualisms, but also distinguishes it from its Graeco-Hellenistic environment.[28] We discern here what has to be the background assumption for the imaginative perception of reality: the temporalization of the world within the horizon of bounded time.

This is undeniably true of the history of Christianity's founding as well. For example, however differently one may characterize the particular modes of believing in early Christianity (for example, the synoptic mode of believing on one hand, the Pauline on another[29]), they all clearly converge in this: they experience and define themselves through an understanding of the world with a horizon of bounded time. What theology will later come to call "imminent expectation" spans the entire New Testament scene. After all, Jesus lived and suffered within its horizon, and Paul formulated his Christology within its understanding of time. Paul's Christology itself is still marked from start to finish by the doctrine of the second coming. Even in Christology it is true: God's having-come is in coming. Pauline Christology is no ideology of historical victors. Paul himself sprinkled temporal elements throughout his Christology. One need only hear, for instance, that "If the dead are not raised, then Christ has not risen" (1 Cor 15:13–16).

What this means, furthermore, is that here the perception of the world within the horizon of bounded time has not yet been surrendered to the gnostic myth of time. Christology and eschatology have not yet been cleanly separated from one another. The apocalyptic sting has not yet been drawn from this eschatology. The Christian understanding of the end times, and its understanding of time in general, have not yet been turned into a gentle, development-minded eschatology. The temporal suspense of hope, its element of expectation, have not yet been exchanged for or semantically twisted into a timeless existential hope (out of the sheer fear of being disappointed). Time as bounded time is still the universal horizon of theology, and the theodicy question is still *the* eschatological question. For this question has not yet been shut down or soothed by theological searches for meaning that are oriented by universal history,[30] by optimistic evolutionary eschatologies,[31] by reduction to gnostic-sounding myths of the identity and authenticity of human existence,[32] by a theology of suffering in God that is too much enclosed and sublated in the Trinity,[33] by too many theologically clever answers to such questions as Who is God? and Where is God? and by too little articulation of the primordial biblical question, What is God waiting for?

The full scope of this understanding of the world, as it structures the biblical discourse on God, can be found in Paul. To be sure, the whole *corpus paulinum* is not to be reduced to one common denominator; he also has statements that are reminiscent of gnosticism, and it is not entirely by chance that later on Marcion will call himself a disciple of Paul. However, the perception of the world in a horizon of bounded time is the dominant one.

But the image of time as bounded did not for Paul mean an emptying or devaluing of the time and reality encountered against its horizon. It is for him by no means an irrelevant transitional time, it is not just time spent in a waiting room. The horizon of bounded time does not at all mean underemphasizing the present; quite the reverse: only in bounded time can the present be experienced in the way Paul emphasizes it. Paul is a missionary. The historical project of Europe (which we have later come to call the Christian West) is inconceivable without him and his missionary activity. Against the horizon of bounded time the world is transformed into an historical world; the experience of time as bounded is the root of the understanding of the world as history, and is the opening act of historical consciousness.

Obviously Paul is no doom-and-gloom fanatic; he does not burden or poison the political landscape with the zealot's heightened dreams of catastrophe. One need only read his sober defense (which we find rather irritating today) of Rome in Romans 13. The horizon of bounded time does not turn us into the voyeurs or the terrorists of our decline. Christianity really became susceptible to totality and agression only after it tried completely to detemporalize its ideas of imminent expectation and second coming by various means—for example, by strict moralization,[34] that is, by transforming eschatology into nothing but ethics. That led to an apocalyptic overburdening of ethical action, which is, in fact, where the dangers of fanaticism and thoughtless praxis lurk.

Pauline discourse about God as a perception and interpretation of the world against the horizon of bounded time does not at all press the end of time upon us with apocalyptic terror. It narrates, remembers and celebrates it as the feast of expectation. Even to this day the confession "...until you come again in glory" stands at the center of our eucharistic cult. But is this celebration still a feast of expectation? Have not Christians too fallen prey long ago to modernity's myth of time, a myth that has robbed us of the capacity to await (one has perhaps only to read this in Beckett)?[35] And has not theology long ago eliminated this "awaiting"— which is a part of the perception of the world within the horizon of bounded time—from its logos, and delegated it to spirituality or liturgy?

V

The danger of detemporalization soon ate away at the soul of Christianity. Of course it is often asserted today that the disappointment of imminent expectation, the fact that the Parousia is still outstanding, did not bring about a fundamental crisis for early Christianity.[36] But in my opinion this assertion overlooks or downplays an important issue. I call it the enduring Marcionite-gnostic temptation of Christian theology, the gnostic wounding of the biblical idea of God. Everyone knows that Marcion came out of Asia Minor during the twilight years of early Christianity, and brought with him a way to deal with the disappointment of imminent expectation and to silence the theodicy question. Against the grain of the biblical way of thinking about God, according to which salvation is not at heart timeless, but has a temporal core, Marcion posited the gnostic axiom of the timelessness of salvation and the irredeemability of time.[37] The intent of this axiom was to disarm once and for all the imminent expectation of early Christianity. Furthermore, he tried to cover the open flank represented by the theodicy question, which accompanies the historical development of the biblical idea of God in the form of complaint, of crying out and of unmollified expectation; he attempted this by means of the gnostic dualism between creator- and redeemer-God. It is certainly true that the early church decisively rejected his approach. It did not even allow Origen's sublime attempt at mediation; instead, it followed Irenaeus, the great anti-Marcionite polemicist. The church refuted Marcion and gnosticism with what we today call universal eschatology.[38] But it did so at a high price. In exchange it got a standing, virtually constitutive danger, the danger of detemporalization, or, speaking more precisely, the standing danger of the temporal bifurcation of eschatology. The concept of time was restricted to biographical and eventually to historical time, but was decoupled from the world's time. Time that is bounded by God's coming, the horizon of God's history, as it is biblically attested, was downplayed more and more or even completely read out of eschatology.

Very early on, if I see things correctly, gnosticism's revenge on Christianity got epistemological reinforcements from the Neoplatonist, Plotinus. His influence, which in Christian philosophy of history reaches at least as far as Hegel, has again and again forced Christian theology under the yoke of an unrelenting identity-thinking. Even the medieval doctrine of analogy was able to assert itself against this tendency only with difficulty. Mediated by Plotinus, the epistemological axiom "like can only be known by like" entered into its anonymous hegemony in Christian theology. But this axiom depicts the highest stage of reflexion as a timeless self-reflection of the absolute.[39] Time has no cognitive worth whatsover. The primordial epistemological axiom for the biblical idea of God, on the other hand, would much more have to be this: Only unlikes can know one another. Surprise, expectation, acceptance, confrontation with the new: all of this belongs to the cognitive structure of a theology committed to the biblical idea of God. Yet the danger of the detemporalization of the Christian logos set in very early. Even before the great foundational Christological and trinitarian discussions of the fourth century, there was a crisis in Christianity's understanding of time, a growing crisis even to this day.[40] Here I would like to give you just a few observations that point to the persistent temptation of Christianity to gnosticism, and its susceptibility to myths (either gnostic or closely related thereto) that downplay the importance of time.

It appears that theology is always in danger of giving up the understanding of time, including time's perception of the world, that is urged upon theology by its biblical heritage, and thereby is in danger of forgetting its own proper word about time: that time is bounded. Theology frequently lives off foreign, borrowed understandings of time, making it questionable how the God of biblical tradition can possibly be thought of in connection with them. This is true of cyclical time, as well as of time sheltered within a cosmos of preestablished harmony, of linear-teleological time. It is true of any progressive continuum, whether it be one that extends into infinitude, evolutionistically empty, or one that is dialectically slowed and interrupted;[41] it is true also of biographically individualized time that is decoupled from nature's and the world's time. And I think it is true of the completely mythical representations of time, which seem to be coming to the fore again. For me, the way that Martin Heidegger has been theologically received is also symptomatic of this forgetfulness of time in theology. He is not received as the one who, with his *Being and Time,* began to analyze the premises of a time-less metaphysics (even if perhaps he did so in the wrong direction); rather, he is recalled as the existential analyst of human existence *[Dasein].*

Presumably the avoidance of time in theology is connected with the fact that theology has always tended, by self-censorship of its biblical idea of God, to free itself from the most offensive of its assertions: imminent expectation and the doctrine of the second coming. Theology either develops argumentative strategies to ignore them altogether, or they are interpreted away or hermeneutically silenced. Yet how otherwise is one supposed to spare oneself the odium of foolishness or incompetency? Thus, for example, in Bultmann's well-known demythologization thesis: "Mythological eschatology is basically finished by the simple fact that Christ's Parousia did not happen immediately as the New Testament expected it to, but that world history continues and—as anyone of sound mind is convinced—will continue."[42] Theology is afraid of not being of sound mind, so in this case it throws itself into the arms of an evolutionistically unbounded time ("which simply continues"). It does so, furthermore, without the slightest suspicion that it could be precisely the myth of time that stands in need of discussion, whose embrace can prove fatal for theology (and not only for it).[43] Even earlier the young Karl Barth had dismissed so-called consistent eschatology, with its emphasis on the outstanding Parousia, by asking sarcastically how something could possibly be outstanding when by its nature it could never come in.[44] As justified as Karl Barth's criticism is of the image whereby Christ's second coming *comes in* within time, just as little does it settle or clarify the theological question of time in general. That would require understanding the doctrine of the second coming in terms of the doctrine of bounded time. Karl Rahner is my ever-present teacher. Nonetheless, I have been troubled by his formulation that "Christ comes again insofar as all things find their way to him."[45] Does this not express a complete detemporalization of time, or the projection of time onto the individual's lifetime?

The most common way by which theology disburdens itself of imminent expectation and the second coming today is by the so-called worldview thesis. One comes right out and consigns both of them to the mythical worldview of archaic biblical time, as if there were some form of Christianity that was devoid of worldview, naked, as it were, as if there were a naked biblical idea of God that one could then dress up, as taste and need require, with different worldviews. But the imaginative grasp of the world against the horizon of bounded time is a nonnegotiable for the biblical idea of God! Or it is so unless one has handed over the idea itself to a myth of time, in the same way that earlier the temporal categories of memory and narrative had been separated out from the logos of theology and consigned to myth. For it is clear that the logos of theology itself must narrate and remember, if it wants to discuss or defend the perception of the world within the horizon of bounded time. In that case the compensation of this logos by myths would not be the decisive task, but rather the winning back of memory and narrative for the logos of theology. This would be especially true of the specifically Christian discourse about God, for when Christology stresses that God has definitively communicated Godself in Jesus Christ, and that God has irrevocably come near to us in Jesus Christ, something is implied about time: *definitively* and *irrevocably*— once and for all—can only be employed against the horizon of bounded time. There is nothing definitive in the horizon of unending time, only the hypothetical. But the logic of bounded time has an anamnestic, a narrative depth structure. And it is in this sense that memory and narrative would have to be won back for the logos of theology. There is an issue in contemporary Christianity on which we can test the success or failure of this task. I would like to conclude with it, since there the theme of *plurality and unity* is present in contemporary Christianity in a particularly controversial way.[46]

VI

After a brief foundational era among Jewish Christians, and a period of almost two thousand years during which it was bound to a relatively uniform cultural sphere (that is, the Western, European world), Christianity today is expanding into a global Christianity taking root in many different cultures. It is on the way from being a culturally monocentric European Christianity to being a culturally polycentric global Christianity. How does theology understand and

come to terms with this ethnic and cultural diversification? Is this
not after all the hour of polymythicism or of a new gnosis in Christianity?[47]

In contemporary theological discussions, the question of the
culturally polycentric global church is treated above all under the
rubric of inculturation. The attempt to protect the real globalization of Christianity from false ethnocentric conclusions, and to
prevent a second power-grab by Europe within the global church,
is often associated with the (gnostic-like) image of a pure or naked
Christianity clothing itself in various cultural garments that are to
some extent secondary to a pregiven identity above time, history
and culture. But this image is a fiction. The culture, which Christianity cannot simply divest itself of like a piece of garment, is the
Western European culture. If movement toward a culturally polycentric global Christianity is not to disintegrate into chaos or into
a polymythic compensation for Europe's lost historical hopes,
then one can hardly overestimate the importance of the self-understanding of European Christianity and its theology.

Obviously European Christianity cannot mature into a culturally polycentric global church by means of that profane Europeanization of the world that we call science, technology and
technological civilization, in terms of which over the last century
Western reason has become practiced in its domination of the
world. Rather, there is growing suspicion that the cultural polycentrism of the world as a whole has already been undermined at
its core by those clearly evident processes through which non-European peoples and cultures are adapting themselves to profane Europeanization, throwing us Europeans (and not a few
European drop-outs among us) back into Eurocentrism
against our will.[48] One also suspects that, through the export of
science and technology, the mythical totality in the background
of European modernity (which we have discussed so much here)
is slowly coming to dominate the world outside Europe as well.
Characterizing this as a danger in no way implies a stupid or
arrogant call for the abolition of our scientific and technological
achievements, nor does it signify an irresponsible wish for the

euthanasia of technology in general. It certainly does indicate, however, a desire for new ways of dealing with those achievements and a desire possibly to set some bounds to so-called modernization processes that are operating more and more automatically. Before we go looking in non-European cultures for answers and reserves for guidance and resistance, we ought to attend to the depth-dimensions of our own culture.

5

Do We Miss Karl Rahner?

Yes, especially given the present situation of our church, both here and around the world, we certainly miss Karl Rahner. We miss him for something we cannot adequately replace, even by sifting through and quoting from his work. In him, work and person, life and theology, were seamlessly one: everything was work, and his work was a unique gesture of Christian existence in our late-modern time. It is this fundamental gesture of his ecclesial, theological and Christian existence that we miss today. This is what I would like to highlight, as we commemorate today his eighty-fifth birthday. For finally, by the time he died, just a few weeks after his eightieth birthday, he had become probably the most important and influential Catholic theologian of his day.

I

The present struggle over the future of the church is governed by different visions that seem almost diametrically opposed. Faced with the widespread crisis of religious identity in our day, which will prevail? Will it be a vision that is turned emphatically toward the past, finally pointing us toward a premodern Western Christendom? Or will another vision assert itself, slowly but persistently, and prove its worth: a vision that will try to save the indispensable inheritance of the Western church in connection with new initiatives in the church (often difficult to comprehend in their entirety) arisen since the last council? It is no accident that this question—at first glance so very abstract—focuses on how to be faithful to this council, on how to save the inheritance of Vatican II.

Karl Rahner's activity at this council constituted an important phase in his life. To be sure, the themes and problems of the post-conciliar church are not simply those of the Second Vatican Council, as Rahner himself stressed on numerous occasions. But he was just as certain that the struggle over the future of the church would be decided by the way this council continued to be present in the life of the church. Will an aggressive or a defensive form of fidelity to this council and retrieval of the church's traditions prevail? Rahner pleaded for an aggressive fidelity.

His aggressive fidelity to the council is supported by a classic Catholic principle for assessing and dealing with the church's tradition, according to which it is not enough to appeal to arbitrarily selected conciliar texts, that is, to maintain an abstract faithfulness to the text, lest one promote a modernization of the church that is just as arbitrary. Rather, for its understanding of fidelity to the council, the classic approach takes into consideration how the church has concretely appropriated this council in the intervening years, particularly how the regional churches have tried to make it bear fruit for their particular situations. In other words, this approach takes as the standard for an understanding of the council its history of effects [Wirkungsgeschichte] within the church. In short, the conciliar tradition that has already formed within the church during the intervening years is the standard for its understanding of the council. One might look at the documents of the Latin American bishops' conferences at Medellín and Puebla, at the postconciliar documents of the Asian bishops, at the episcopal synods in the Federal Republic, or at other comparable events in France, Holland and in the United States. Everywhere the council has been interpreted as an impetus to new initiatives and to courageous self-reform. Following the classic Catholic understanding, therefore, would not aggressive fidelity have to be the attitude, the hermeneutic lens (as it were) with which we read and interpret the conciliar texts?

While the model of the church from the First Vatican Council is still clearly formed in terms of the relationship between sovereign and subject, it is well known that the biblical image of the pilgrim people of God is the most prominent one in the last council's understanding of the church. And since this council, the people of God—on strong biblical grounds—have been testing out this new path. Certainly this is not an easy thing to learn, and does not come without stumbling, indeed without getting lost or wandering off the path. But as one should never discourage a child from learning to walk just because everyone knows falling down is a part of the process, neither should the church keep the faithful from this new way of walking one's own path just because of the risks inherent in it. Whoever would save, must venture risk. Rahner called this aggressive form of fidelity to the council, and to the tradition in general, a "rigorism of the venture." This distinguishes him just as much from a zealously intense traditionalism and fundamentalism as it does from a liberalism that is all too ready to adapt itself. It allows him to understand the council not as an end, but rather as the germinal beginning of a beginning that will yield the praxis for a new epoch of church history, both here in Europe and worldwide: the venturing toward a culturally polycentric global church and the irrupting of the poor church into the heart of the church's life.

Since then, the impulse toward new ventures and the readiness for reform have been paralyzed. A defensive mentality, demanding certainty and an emphatically defensive way of preserving traditions, seems to be spreading from Rome outward into the whole Church. Such defensive rigorism focuses principally on the complex difficulties and contradictions that come up in ventures of this sort, which certainly ought not to be dismissed. Tensions between the church and so-called modernity, which have been smoldering for centuries, are breaking into the open; a repressed Enlightenment, which we thought we had overcome without really passing through it with open eyes, is continually pressing its claims on us. The fact that Catholicism is out of step with the times presents not only opportunities, but tragedies as well, tragedies that must be lived through, suffered through. But how?

With a defensive and exclusionary mentality obsessed with certitude? Or with a mentality that, some years ago when discussing the heritage of the council, I called the "reformers' second courage"? Indeed, real renewal does not happen simply in the heads and hearts of bishops and theologians gathered at council. It may certainly begin there, with the first courage of proclaiming renewal or new ventures and self-reform. But renewal requires a second courage of the bishops and theologians, as well as of the people of God invoked on its authority. This is the courage of concrete imagination, of concrete engagement, when questions and difficulties boil up. For the truth of renewal only becomes a living truth when it becomes the truthfulness of the church and the credibility of believers themselves, where it finds its ground in the transformed community of believers. I see in Karl Rahner a prototype of such a second courage.

Second courage is reflected again and again in Rahner's postconciliar work. More than almost anyone else, he saw the concrete questions men and women had after the Council, and was without equal in the way he made himself accountable to them. Indeed, his obedience to this accountability became virtually the tacit organizational principle of his multifarious later writings. At issue here is not whether all his suggestions and concerns were in every case germane; he was probably not even sure of this himself. What is crucial are the ways in which he articulated a second courage, and it is for these we miss him. His expressions certainly did not always make him friends, not in Rome, not among bishops, and not among his colleagues. To be specific, I remember his little book *The Shape of the Church to Come*,[1] which offered suggestions for the 1972 synod of German bishops and, in the spirit of the council, attempted to point a path toward renewal of the church's life, both in Germany and throughout the world.

When he boldly laid out in this book the outlines of a *church from below*, and even spoke of a democratic church, he was not questioning the duality of office and community; that is, he was not suggesting that ecclesial office could be deduced or derived from the people of the church. Rather what was important for him was a new, living coordination of the two. He was concerned about something that even in Rome is willingly named *communion* and *participation* in the church's life, terms which hardly anyone would use to describe the present Roman practices of appointing bishops and dealing with local churches. Ecclesial renewal cannot be impressed from above into the souls of the faithful!

His second courage led Rahner also to speak of a culture of freedom of conscience in the church. He really understood the conciliar decree on religious freedom to be the first attempt to connect the *rights of the truth* indissolubly with the *rights of persons in their truth*. In this way, according to Rahner, the church would escape its everpresent temptation "to want to triumph by detouring around the consciences of men and women." It goes without saying that the appeal to freedom of conscience did not for Rahner mean opening the doors to arbitrariness or relativism. For who more than he had concerned himself for years—as a dogmatic theologian!—with questions in moral theology? Yet it was precisely his painstaking treatment of these questions that led him also to speak of a "church of morality without moralizing." In the overmoralization of ecclesial life, he saw the danger that the church would separate itself from the heart of its message. In *The Shape of the Church to Come* he said:

> We must show men and women today at least the beginning of the path that leads credibly and concretely into the freedom of God. Where men and women have not begun to have the experience of God and of God's Spirit, who liberates us from the most profound anxieties of life and from guilt, there is no point in proclaiming to them the ethical norms of Christianity. Indeed, they would not be able to understand them; at most they would be for them only the source of still more radical constraints and even deeper anxiety.[2]

In this context Rahner warns against an all-too-extravagant use of doctrinal casuistry in contemporary doctrinal pronouncements, and stresses that

God does not take our worldly problems from us, he does not spare us our bewilderment. Thus, we should not act in the church as if God did. In the final analysis even our appeals to God casts us into an ultimate bewilderment....One comes to terms with this ultimate bewilderment only as, in a holy "agnosticism" before God, one surrenders oneself hopefully and lovingly to this inconceivable God, who never guaranteed that all our calculations would work out smoothly if only we got along well with God.[3]

Later, in considering an all-too-moralistic church, which is always pointing out human sinfulness, Rahner tactfully asks us to consider whether there must not also be room in the church's proclamations and spirituality for humans to complain and to turn their questioning back to God when they are faced with the horrors in God's creation.

In the same book Rahner also presses for an *open church,* not open to arbitrariness, not open in a vague or unfocused sense, but rather open in opposition to a mentality that is gaining ground today, one that wants to close itself off, a sectarian mentality in the church. In my view, this is increasingly becoming a question of the very future of the church. For the church is in the midst of a very complex process that in some ways pulls in virtually opposite directions. On one hand the church finds itself, in Rahner's words, on the verge of becoming a truly global church, in which what was promised in the earliest history of the church is becoming tangible for the first time: "You will be my witnesses to the ends of the earth" (Acts 1:8). On the other hand, it is clear that through this very same process the church, here and worldwide, is becoming a minority. On a global scale it is finding itself in a diaspora, biblically speaking, in exile. This is true all over the globe, and not least in Europe. Yet a sect is defined in a theological sense by its possession of a certain mentality, not by the number of its members. The church need be neither ashamed nor afraid of being a minority, unless one holds that the church is the inner-worldly executor of the universal history of salvation to which it witnesses. But this would be to misunderstand the history of salvation as an ideology of history that has replaced the

church's genuine hope, and in which the eschatological difference between the church and the reign of God has been suppressed. Rather, the church should fear the symptoms of a
creeping sectarian mentality, to which Rahner directed his own
reflections as well: the trend toward fundamentalism, toward a
pure traditionalism; the growing unwillingness or inability to
embrace new experiences and incorporate them by painful and
critical assimilation into the church's self-understanding; a zealously charged language and an unempathetic militancy in inner-
ecclesial confrontations; the transformation of our sense for
church into joyless and humorless zealotry; increasing and widespread pressures toward excessive loyalty, or symptoms of para-
noia in ecclesial life; the pressure to associate only with the
like-minded; the danger of an artificial isolation of the language
of proclamation, turning it into a purely in-house language with
typically sectarian semantics. Rahner contested all of this with the
virtually mystical power of his optimism concerning salvation. He
was always a universalist, who would never allow the church to
turn the God it proclaimed into its own private property. His
Ignatian pathos for the ever-greater God would never permit him
any sectarian-sounding church piety.

Furthermore, Rahner often asked whether or not much of the
interconfessional strife in Christianity bore these kinds of sectarian
characteristics. Here his plea for an ecumenical church may serve
as a final example of his second courage. As early as 1972 (once
again in *The Shape of the Church to Come*), when the ecumenical
movement in our nation threatened to stagnate, Rahner made this
bold proposal: "Up to this point...we have tried to tackle the question of union in its theological and confessional dimensions, and
have seen institutional union merely as the consequence of clearing up controversial theological issues. But could we not take the
opposite tack? Could we not think of the complete unity in faith
and theology as a consequence of institutional unification, particularly since this would not have to mean...institutional uniformity?"[4]
In 1978 the elderly Rahner outlined in his "Dream of the Church"
an image of the Petrine office which, without surrendering the

defined substance of this office, would no longer have to pose an obstacle for inner-Christian ecumenism; and just one year before his death, in a book co-authored with Heinrich Fries, he tried to elaborate this vision of the Petrine office in light of the so-called *ex cathedra* decisions of the pope.[5]

My suspicion is that here again it is Rahner's pathos for God that forms the background of his second courage for ecumenism, his pathos for a God who is near, but yet in his most intimate nearness still hidden and thus also easy to overlook. This God-pathos binds Rahner to the God-pathos of Ignatius, the founder of his order, and with that of Martin Luther as well, whose passion for God probably only looks so opposed to that of Ignatius because of apologetic clichés.

II

All this points toward the religious roots of Rahner's second courage, to which we now turn our attention. When we do, we immediately encounter another fundamental characteristic of his theological personality, another reason why we miss him. I call this the charism of his critical freedom in the church. Second courage cannot be had without the courage to criticize, without the courage of timely objection and opposition. Now Rahner (in good Jesuit fashion) was virtually born a man of the church, as it were, an *anima naturaliter ecclesiastica*. He always understood his passionate critique of conditions in the church and its authorities as a saving critique. Rahner never toyed with the church, he never used it as a stage or window dressing for his private theology. He never thought of the church as some sort of collective virtuoso performance in which one is supposed to become intoxicated; an aesthetic relationship to the church was quite foreign to him. And cynicism in general, regarding the church in particular, was profoundly alien to him. Once I tried to interpret his cries of complaint in this way: Rahner lived the church in his belly. Thus when it failed, he felt it there, like a colic. And who then would not cry out?

Such crying out absolutely deserves a hearing, should not too quickly be toned down. It does not come from the outside. Rahner's immanent critique on quite specific situations in the church has a mystical root; in the final analysis it is provoked by the passionate question of whether and how God himself, God's unspeakable mystery, is released and empowered in the church. His critique therefore fights against all the ways that the church is tempted to want to forget its own eschatological provisionality and to replace the liberating mystery of God with itself. All those who would rashly trace critical protest in the church or a growing weariness with the church back to an unecclesial modern unbelief, should be measured by his critique of the church.

And finally also by what I would call—Rahner would never admit this—his authority. For this too we miss him. Here I do not mean his competency for educating and arguing; nor that easygoing authority that derived from Rahner's naiveté, which, to be sure, did not express any uncertainty or hesitancy, but rather a particular sort of mastery that led him to pose childlike questions and break out of the all-too-well-trodden ways of understanding things. We ought to spend a great deal more time speaking of this authority of his, since it had nothing at all to do with elitism or the esoteric, and had about it nothing of the air of a master-thinker. No, here I am thinking exclusively of the theological authority which derived from his religious competence.

On the twenty-fifth anniversary of his ordination, some of his first students (including Herbert Vorgrimler and myself) gave Karl Rahner a wristwatch which he wore until his death, and upon which was engraved "1 Cor 4:15." That is where Paul says, "You certainly have many teachers in Christ, but few fathers." Rahner had become for us not only a teacher, but a father of faith, a brother in faith. Precisely because of this he became for us, and for many, a productive example of how to deal theologically with what is probably the most profound crisis facing contemporary Christianity: the crisis of passing on the faith to the next generation, from old to young. In my opinion it is in this crisis that the impact of our post-modern times upon the life of the church and of Christians in general is most clearly evident. In a time of profound crisis of intact, that is, life-defining traditions; in a time in which a progressive loss of memory threatens to become the paradigm for authentic progress; in a time in which the computer, which cannot remember anything, indeed because it forgets nothing, is increasingly replacing memory; in a (postmodern) time in which, to be sure, history continually runs up against interest not because it is accountable to it, but rather because, transformed into literature, it neutralizes it: in such times Rahner becomes an example of how we can—even now, even still—pass on the faith that has been handed down to us. Of course this is connected with perhaps the most decisive achievement of his theology, which I would like in conclusion to describe.

III

I have said that life and work were one in Rahner. His theology was a unique gesture of Christian existence in postmodern times. In other words, he brought together in his theology what has been divided for a long time. For Catholic theology in modernity has been (as Urs von Balthasar pointed out decades ago) stamped by a profound schism between doctrine and life, between theological system and religious experience, between theology and religion, between dogmatics and mysticism, between the doxography and biography of Christian existence. I do not mean by this that in modern theology individual theologians have not also been pious. Here I am not thinking of a private reconciliation of doctrine and one's life story, but rather of the fact that such reconciliation itself never became theology, that it did not attain communicatively a public character, that it acquired so little weight for the destiny of faith in the modern age.

Things could go on this way tolerably well as long as society itself retained a religious character, and as long as theology had not yet lost its public capacity to generate consensus. But at least since the Enlightenment and what followed, the bifurcation became ever more evident and the schism had ever more disastrous effects. Religious experience, the articulation of one's life story before God, fell theologically more and more by the wayside, so that increasingly theology dismantled the contents of its experience in a subjectivistic or impressionistic way (like some sort of psychology of faith). Consequently, theology has become less and less able to bring its experience to bear in the public sphere of ecclesial and social life, or convincingly to resist the prejudice against religion and religious experience that germinated in the ideology critique of an earlier time and has since become deeply embedded in the general consciousness. So-called real theology, and above all dogmatics, has in fact turned more and more into objectivistically stunted doctrine and often functioned as a systematized anxiety concerning life beyond its concepts, a life that has profound depths.

Consequently, many contemporary theologians have turned completely away from doctrine; in the name of life and of experience, they criticize the strongly doctrinal side of Christianity. They separate religion from doctrinal theology in order to give back to religious experience its proper dignity and in order finally to offer nourishment, the bread of life, to that secret hunger for consolation which not even the Enlightenment's critique of religions has been able to satisfy or eliminate. They try to lead Christianity out of the realm of history and its contradictions and into the realm of myth; they try to unlock the potential for consolation that slumbers in myths and fables. In so doing they have found a great deal of receptivity in an ever-more-bewildered and experientially impoverished Christianity. They call our attention to Jesus' therapeutic manner and exempt him once and for all from the dilemma between doctrine and life. To counter the moral overburdening of men and women by Christian doctrine, they fall back on the soothing power of myth and its supposition of human innocence. They point out how much free-floating, helplessly vagrant anxiety there is in our late modern age, and how neither the church nor professional theology knows what to do with this anxiety. In this way they have put their finger correctly on a painful consequence of the modern schism in theology. Yet at what price? A theology that has despaired of doctrine and, in the name of religion, bids farewell to history and to its tension between the mystical and the political, easily turns into an edifying psychology with a postmodern touch. But Christians, with their religious experience, continue to be accountable to concrete history no matter what; the canon of doctrine itself turns on concrete history—"suffered under Pontius Pilate"—and doctrine itself presses upon Christians the experience of that history in which there is crucifixion, torture, massacre, tears, love and hate. No myth can soothe them and restore them to the innocence they have lost in such a history; at any rate, that is what a Christianity involved in life teaches.

In my opinion, Rahner's life work has succeeded in bringing together what has long been separated, indeed set at variance: his work has brought to an end the schism between theology and life history; it has related doctrine and life, the mystical and the everyday, in the context of the irreducible complexity and anonymity of our postmodern situation. To be sure, throughout the history of Christian theology, even in modernity, there have been important individual theologians in whom doctrine and life history have been brought into impressive and moving synthesis: not only in Augustine, the prototype of such theology, but also with Pascal and Newman, with Kierkegaard and Bonhoeffer, to name only the best known. But Rahner's synthesis is of another sort, and precisely because of this it is in a particularly promising way "contemporary."

In distinction to their famous biographical theologies, Rahner's theology is in some measure the mystical biography of the ordinary, the average Christian person; it is the attempt to spell out, in the canon of doctrines, a Christian life without great transformations and turning points, without special illuminations and conversions: in short, it is the biographical theology of an expressly antibiographical type. With Rahner it is not the great, dramatically stirred subjectivity that dominates in theology

and christens it biographical; rather, in him it becomes clear
how traditional doctrine can be connected to and expressed
precisely in the experience of the everyday in its height and
depth, in its tribulations and its hopes. Here *great* is an inappro-
priate, romantic category. Everything is unpretentious, but also
and precisely because of this, exemplary. And thus it came
about that, despite the oft-lamented difficulty of his language,
he was close to the multitudes; without being condescending or
patronizing, he was able to guess at and discuss much that was
bewildering, especially (as he grew older) for the younger generation. This was not at all an attempt to pour interpretations of
religious experience "from above" into bewildered souls; rather,
it worked because it was an invitation to a journey of discovery
into the virtually uncharted territory of one's own life, and that
is why it worked.

Such a confluence of the world of faith and the world of life,
of the mystical and the profane everyday, can less and less be
prefabricated by the individual theologian. New places and
new subjects for theological endeavor must come to the fore, if
this reconciliation of doctrine and life is to succeed in the
future. Rahner himself prepared an understanding of theology
that absolutely permitted speaking of a theological authority
and the dignity of the ordinary Christian woman and man. In
the final analysis the language of faith is exhausted by neither
the instructional language of the shepherds nor the arguments
of the theological experts! Did not the last council emphasize
that we should see the faithful not primarily as objects but as
subjects, not as addressees but as the bearers of faith and its
memory of God? Does this not mean a new dignity and authority, a new maturity *[Mündigkeit]* for ordinary believers in the
church? a new maturity not only in view of the profane life
world, but also in view of the world of faith? And do we not
have good reasons since the council to say that really there
must be, alongside the teaching office of the church, something like a teaching authority of believers in the church—in
order to achieve something like an enrichment of the language

of faith by drawing from life-histories? At my urging, Rahner's next theological contribution was supposed to deal with this question. His death intervened.

Here, it seems to me, is one of the main questions to be dealt with if this fundamental intention of Rahner's life work—his integration of doctrine and life—is to be satisfied, especially under today's new and more difficult conditions. It is clear that an absolutely essential presupposition for believers becoming subjects in theology is that we get rid of a patronizing caretaker-mentality in the life of the church. But I wonder if this is going to happen, not only when I look at the contemporary situation of the church, but also at the social context from which Christian faith can never quite manage to divorce itself. Do we not see in that social context a new and growing privatization, spread through gentle seduction by our modern culture industry? Is there not a kind of weariness at being a subject; trained to fit in, do we not think in terms of little niches? Is there not a growing spectator mentality with no obligation to perceive critically, a rather voyeuristic way of dealing with social and political crises? Are there not in our secularized and enlightened world signs of a second immaturity *[Unmündigkeit]*, fed by the experience that more than ever before we are informed about everything, especially about what threatens us and about all the horrors in the world, but that the step from knowledge to action, from consciousness of crisis to dealing with crisis, has never seemed so great and so unlikely to occur as it does today? Does not such experience dispose us not to action but to resignation, a new readiness in our profane world to be watched over and taken care of? When this trend breaks into the life of the church, it stabilizes yet again a traditionalistically oriented caretaker-church, a church that watches over us from above—contrary to the promise of a new beginning in the council. For a traditionalistic caretaker-church is what really conforms to the "spirit" of the age!

We should not deceive ourselves about this situation, nor about the difficulties that await us if we try to follow the trail that

Rahner blazed for the life of the church and of theology. It is on this journey toward a church that does not fit in, that respects the dignity and authority of believers and the theological integrity of all men and women, that we will probably most miss him.

6

Karl Rahner's Struggle for the Theological Dignity of Humankind

When Karl Rahner died ten years ago in Innsbruck, within a month of his eightieth birthday, he was probably the most significant and influential Catholic theologian of his time, and a powerful inspiration and challenge to his church. And if Catholic theology today sees differently or farther than he, that is because he pushed it to the intellectual heights of the age as hardly any other before him. Despite this background presence, and despite the fact that for some time many of his insights and expressions have lived on in common theological usage without explicit attribution, for many today he seems distant, strange and unfamiliar. Perhaps he has become foreign to us in precisely those areas in which we ought to miss his presence; perhaps he is unfamiliar and distant precisely in those places where he could be an adviser and a productive mentor in this our time of need.

For how can one engage in theology today—theology not in this or that sense, but rather as discourse about God? How does one formulate it and hand it on today, within this postmodern welter of tongues and voices, in our increasingly confusing and traditionless situation? Rahner's theology was not really dominated by a classical canon of questions that could be tidily summed up into a system; rather, his theology submitted itself to the canon of life's questions. It was not those carefully chosen in advance, but the disquieting questions, the importunate, often frighteningly profane questions that he allowed to lay claim to him, even to the point of exhaustion. This conjoining of life's questions and the questions of faith, this overcoming of the schism between life and doctrine, between the mystical and the everyday in the impenetrable complexity and anonymity of our situation, is the leitmotif of his theology; furthermore, it tells us something crucial about his *system*. It is no accident that his system eludes description in extensive monographs or popular paperbacks.

Just as obviously, Rahner understood himself to be accountable to the *Catholic* vision of Christianity, that is, to Christianity as church. Though deeply rooted in his church, he tried time and again to open it up and move beyond it to the intellectual and spiritual situation of his time. In this regard a bland liberalism was just as foreign to him as a zealously sharpened fundamentalism, with its doctrinaire and moralizing casuistry. He felt himself bound up with the church's traditions in a kind of aggressive fidelity: Whoever wants to preserve, must risk. He understood the last council—which is indebted to him for some of its pivotal theological impulses—as the beginning of a beginning. With the intellectual courage of his convictions, he struggled in his church for the ineluctable authority of all believers and the theological dignity of all humankind.

In considering this theme we immediately encounter a fundamental feature of the way Rahner engaged in theology: the never trivial, but rather creative naiveté with which he questioned the prevailing ecclesial consensus; the penetrating gaze with which he remembered and retrieved, in an almost subversive way, things supposedly long gone or forgotten. A series of essays in *Theological Investigations* proposed rethinking the Second Vatican Council in a productive way.[1] In the midst of the postconciliar euphoria, Rahner—to whom, as already mentioned, the council owes important theological initiatives—never lost sight of the difficult passage looming on the horizon. Thus his critique in no way came merely from the outside, but rather from within the church's history of teaching and learning itself: for it was also an education in how to work with forgotten truths. He confronted statements from the Second Vatican Council with doctrinal assertions from the

First Vatican Council of 1869–70. That council is, rightly enough, considered a precarious one, due to the feudal model of the church dominating its background; yet in the narrower theological sense, in its dealing with the question of God, it was to no small degree an explosive one.

In the above-mentioned texts, Rahner draws our attention to the fact that the Second Vatican Council no longer talked about God, as Vatican I still had, but rather confined itself to the God announced in and by the church. Rahner sees a questionable immunizing tendency at work here, to some extent an ecclesiological enciphering of talk about God, in order to avoid from the very start the God-crisis that tacitly prevails among us. But for Rahner God is a universal theme, a theme concerning all humanity, or it simply is no theme at all. God is never for him the private property of the church, nor of theology. And not even of faith: the lightning flash of God is to be reckoned on every human experiential and linguistic terrain. So Rahner questions the ecclesiological enciphering of discourse about God in the last council: Is it not symptomatic of a church that is becoming a sect, and symptomatic of the growing cognitive isolation of theology in our society?

THE HUMAN APTITUDE FOR GOD AND THE THEOLOGICAL COMPETENCE THAT DERIVES FROM IT

But what does an appeal to Vatican I mean in this context? In what follows, concerning the human aptitude[2] for God and human theological competence, I am not certain how far I can refer explicitly to Karl Rahner's texts. There are, to be sure, occasional passing remarks, and these indicate precisely by their casual character just how deeply rooted they are in Rahner's thought.

First, one reference shows that even in his later years Rahner never lost sight of the First Vatican Council. This is from the thirteenth volume of his *Investigations:*

This council, disparaged by so many today, has, correctly understood, turned out to be a great council, despite all the fustiness that naturally prevailed among the council fathers, horrified at their age, who at best wanted to return to the age before the Enlightenment and French Revolution. A magnificent council. Why? Because it clarified the natural knowability of God by means of the light of reason alone.[3]

Here we are not speaking of a mere provisional conciliar statement, but rather of a doctrinal definition the church has raised to the level of dogma. The definition states: "The Holy Mother Church asserts and teaches: God, ground and goal of all things, can be known with certainty from created things with the natural light of human reason" (DS 3026).

For the most part, given the intellectual situation of the time, and not least in view of ecumenical dialogue with Lutheran theology, this definition gives Catholic theology a headache. Consequently it would gladly pass over it in silence or relativize it with torturous explanations. But I see in it something that Karl Rahner also clearly valued. This definition counters any attempt to encipher discourse about God too quickly within a theology of revelation or even within the church, due to a kind of theological despair in modern men and women and their aptitude for God.

Critics of the definition will insist that here we have a case in which the council itself stumbled into the very rationalism it was trying to combat; that here the council subscribed to a typically rationalistic overestimation of human reason. Others will stress that the council was not making a statement about human reason and its powers, but rather about a proposition of faith: that Christian faith in a creator God can never be contrary to reason. Of course, the question remains open here as to what sort of reason faith cannot contradict. The definition of reason continues to be controversial, and in this controversy the church itself may not put claim upon any particular concept of reason, lest its definition end up being nothing but a tautology.

Another variant of the critique, suspicious of ideology, sounds particularly plausible to many today. The suspicion: in an age when the church's dogma was no longer considered universally binding, the church tried to win back in an underhanded way such universally binding character, such universal competence, by appeal to a natural knowledge of God. In other words, the definition was a way of trying to expand its jurisdiction again to include all men and women. Thus the doctrine of a natural knowledge of God is ultimately unveiled to be a sort of compensation for loss of jurisdiction. The definition is regarded as an expression of a belated intellectual imperialism in the Catholic Church, which pretends to have overcome the Enlightenment without having passed through it. For these critics of the definition, moreover, the Catholic Church deals with natural law the same way it deals with reason: setting itself up as the guardian of universal and inalienable natural law, it tries to win back in questions of morality and social ethics that universal jurisdiction it long ago had lost with its dogmas.

The best way to meet this widely shared critique is to follow an approach to the evaluation of the First Vatican Council that I see laid out, at least indirectly, by Karl Rahner. In this view the definition is not talking primarily about the competence of the church, but about the natural competence of all human beings in matters concerning God. The matter of which Christianity speaks from its core, even today in the continuing process of the Enlightenment and in the widely heralded diffusion of postmodernism—that is, the God of which it speaks—is a fundamental matter on which everyone can join in the conversation and on which therefore everyone must be heard. So this dogma is not only or primarily trying to impose an obligation on unbelievers, but rather on the church, on theology and on believers themselves. The church and theology must stand ready, in whatever concerns its God, to converse with everyone, to listen to everyone, to argue with everyone who cannot in advance be denied having reason and good will— that is, who cannot be regarded from the start as stupid or evil. (Here it might be worthwhile to refer to parallel dealings by the church with the idea of natural law—especially in view of the recent encyclical *Veritatis Splendor*. Murder, torture and artificial birth control are indiscriminately listed on the same level as "intrinsically evil acts." Given this, if the church intends to talk about universal natural law today, it can only look upon the majority of humankind as evil in Augustinian terms, as a *massa damnationis,* since the majority of humankind refuses to reject artificial birth control and place it as an evil of equal moral weight with murder, genocide and torture.)

Thus the doctrinal definition of Vatican I can quite legitimately be understood as opposing an ecclesiological enciphering of the competence we have for God and of our discussion about God. Even if it remains an open question as to what the council fathers themselves intended—and they argued violently with one another—the doctrinal definition can still be understood as a statement in which the church is not primarily seeking to empower and authorize itself in issues concerning God, but rather one in which it exposes itself and shows an open flank for the painful and contradictory historical experience of humanity. It can be understood as a statement in which the church reminds its own teaching authority to respect the competence and authority of *others* in its talk about God. This doctrinal statement is a stimulus to a new and elementary respect for all men and women when it comes to talking about God. It requires of the church, above all, that when it talks about God it respect the authority of those who suffer, that it not pass over the language and cries of despair, the negative theology, so to speak, in the human history of suffering, but rather that it make them its teacher for speaking about God. (Why is it that this history of humanity's suffering is so little seen or heard when Christians talk about God?) This doctrinal statement demands that Christian language about God listen even to discourse which denies God, and not dismiss it as beneath the level of its own doubts. To put it somewhat boldly, what we have in this doctrinal statement from Vatican I is a kind of "declaration of human rights": the right of rational persons of good will to be heard (and not just to be instructed) when it comes to the God-question. It is a matter of the human right of the aptitude of all men and women for God, even of so-called modern men and women. For, repeating myself and following

Karl Rahner's sense, God is either a theme for all humanity, or it is no theme at all!

Rahner has the following ecclesial axiom: all persons who are not excluded in advance because they are irrational or of evil will, must be heard, must absolutely be heard and taken extremely seriously. Therefore in his theology it is not simply a systematically preestablished canon of questions that predominates; rather, it is the canon of those life questions which have been brought to it from all sides and from out of the most profound this-sidedness, and to which it submits itself for God's sake, even to the point of exhaustion. This, if I see it correctly, is his contribution to overcoming the crisis of meaning and tradition in Christianity that is so often conjured up today. And I know of no greater contribution that any theologian could make.

Rahner made intellectual sacrifices to his impressive theological universalism. Here I refer, very briefly, to his variously received and much-discussed theory of anonymous Christianity. The theory—if one wants to call it that—is clearly marked by two of Rahner's fundamental convictions. The first is the central theological idea of an invincible, universal salvific will of God, to which Rahner was passionately committed, and which aligns Rahner much more closely with Origen than Augustine. The second is a humane respect for the hidden depths of human existence, which are unavailable to absolute reflection, and in which human beings finally remain anonymous and enigmatic even to themselves. If this notion enabled Rahner truly to see Christians in all persons of good will (and could also equally suggest that there are unchristian atheists within the church), this was not because of a tendency to claim all men and women for Christianity; rather, it was guided much more by an incipient tendency within Christianity itself, especially in his church. In talking about anonymous Christianity, he was trying to communicate a sense of the breadth of God and the narrowness of the church. With it he fought against the growing despair on the part of the church toward modern men and women; he tried to prevent the church's fear of coming into contact with the modern world from drifting into a sectarian mentality in which confessing Christians instinctively deal with and seek consensus only among themselves.

Nonetheless, in its philosophical-theological groundings this theory has enkindled the critical objection I have against the transcendental theological paradigm in general.[4] I will not press the critique strongly here, because despite it I still consider myself in agreement with Rahner's option. Perhaps one or two informal remarks. First: If one follows his theory then everyone, everyone who is not explicitly Christian, would have to be able to be an anonymous Christian. But that is not right. It is not true for the Jews, not for Israel, which—according to Paul—has a salvific significance of its own, with its proper meaning, alongside Christianity and for it, "until the end" (see Rom 9–11). Is not the theory of an anonymous Christianity based then upon an ahistorical understanding of universality, the universality of Christianity? It comes from a transcendental philosophy of consciousness that can neither think of nor thoughtfully defend the eschatological differences in Christianity. And a second critical remark: must not the theory of anonymous Christianity operate too much with the principle of *bona fides* ("You are certainly good, but you understand yourself falsely.")? Does not this principle remain too closely connected to a precritical, pre-Enlightenment paradigm of consciousness, which in view of the Enlightenment's ideal of maturity *[Mündigkeit]* cannot avoid arousing the suspicion that it has been fabricated in order to preempt others' arguments and pacify them? Today's man or woman refuses to be interpreted in a way that is fundamentally against his or her own convictions.

THE LANGUAGE OF PRAYER

That observation brings me back once again to Rahner, to an important impulse present in his stressing of the theological dignity of men and women. I can make it clearer in this way. Only theoretical naiveté could make modern theologians think they can ground their language—that is, their discourse about God—in the modern spheres of epistemology and linguistic theory. All these theories—not only logical positivism but also, for example, discourse and communication theories—are, to say the least, methodologically atheistic; they are at best linguistic theories in which the word "God" can no longer be found. Hardly anyone knew better than Karl Rahner that all discourse *about* God has an authentic linguistic base only insofar as it is rooted in a discourse *with* God, that is, that the theoretically indispensable linguistic realm for theology is the language of prayer. Hence the characteristic oscillation in Rahner between the language of prayer and the language of argumentation, between mystagogy and theology, between spirituality and theological intellectuality, which some superficial theologies liked to reproach in him as dilettantism.

Yet—and Rahner knew this, even if he did not explicitly make use of the argument—the language of prayer is much more universal than the language of scientific *[wissenschaftlichen]* theology in the academy. The discipline of religious studies confirms this fact. Occasionally it will speak of a "monotheism of prayer," even in polytheistic religions; but the language of prayer is not only more universal, it is also more alive and dramatic, more rebellious and more radical than the language of academic theology. It is much more troubling, unconsoled, much less harmonized. Have we ever really understood what has accumulated through the centuries of the history of religion in this language of prayer: the crying out and the jubilation, lament and song, the doubt and the mourning, even the final falling into silence? Have we Christians perhaps not oriented ourselves too much by the liturgically and ecclesially managed language of prayer, and have we perhaps been nourished so much by instances gleened too one-sidedly from biblical traditions, that we can no longer hear and recognize how much the language of prayer is found among the children of men? The language of prayer is finally a language without taboos, and yet at the same time a language filled with painful discretion. It does not condemn the ineffably addressed to answer, to enter into the friendly I-thou. It is not entertaining conversation. It cannot be described as either dialogue or com-

munication in the familiar sense, and so it cannot be made perfectly intelligible by either a discourse theory or a philosophy of
communication. It endures as the seedbed of negative theology;
it remains the place where the prohibition of images is practiced.
It perdures as the defenseless refusal to allow itself to be consoled
by ideas or myths; it is that passion for and of God, very often
nothing else than a wordless sigh of the creature. Or, to borrow
here a phrase that Rahner frequently employed: a crying out for
the light of God.

The language of prayer is much more comprehensive than the
language of belief; in it one can even say that one does not
believe. It is the most peculiar and yet the most widespread language of the children of men; it is a language that would have no
name, if there were not the word *prayer*. It is the language of the
human competence for God, into which Rahner's universalism
(this, at any rate, is how I understand it) would lure us. It is a language that we can hear and experience only after we break open
(with Rahner) the all too zealous ecclesiological and theological
encipherment of discourse about God and of prayer.

THE NONTRANSFERABLE NEGATIVE MYSTERY
OF HUMAN SUFFERING

To say it at the start, in brief and concise form: Rahner's hesitation, indeed, his refusal, to talk of a suffering God has something
to do with his fundamental theological respect for the suffering
and the history of suffering of humanity. The sphere to which the
theme of God and suffering belongs is, in scholastic terminology,
that of the theodicy question. Rahner hardly ever expressed himself explicitly on that question (which in itself should of course
give us something to think about); neither did he deal with the
form of the question already brought into sharp focus in fundamental theology: How are we to speak at all of God, given the
abysmal history of suffering in a world that nonetheless must be
considered God's good creation? But when he does broach this
question, as in his short essay in one of the later volumes of *Theo-*

logical Investigations, "Why Does God Allow Us to Suffer?", his penetrating vision and the way his questioning subverts established notions and answers are immediately apparent.[5]

Why does God allow us to suffer? Rahner will not avail himself of the usual response given in theology—"suffering stems from sin, and God must permit sin for the sake of human freedom." As he asks in this short essay,

> For what does "permitting" mean when we are talking about a God who is purely and simply the ground and cause of all reality, who, moreover, in the absolute sovereignty of his freedom and power, is in no way restricted by anyone or anything, encompasses all creaturely freedom and does not come up against any limit there?…What does "permitting" mean, if according to the theology (particularly that of the classical schools) of the relationship between divine and human freedom there can be no doubt that God, without in any way infringing or diminishing the freedom of the creature, in his predestination could so forestall creaturely freedom that in practice sin as "no" to his holy will did not occur in the world…?[6]

Rahner was also aware of the question Romano Guardini is said to have asked on his deathbed: "Why, God, these fearful detours on the way to salvation, why the suffering of the innocent, why sin?"[7] For my part, I would call this question the primary and genuine theodicy question, and I would characterize it—here, without being able to appeal to Rahner—as *the* eschatological question, for which theology must not come up with an answer but must always, and in every new situation, find and elaborate a language.

In the final volume of his *Schriften zur Theologie,* which appeared the year he died, Rahner took up once again and for the last time the question of the relationship between the church's teachings and the "piety of the common people."[8] Here we see him troubled by ecclesial teachings and pronouncements that, faced with situations in creation that cry out to heaven, only and always admonish and question human conduct but do not

show, as I would say, a "concern about God." Rahner himself asks
if the observation that "men and women do not so much feel
themselves guilty before God, as they require that God justify
himself for the horrible state of the world which God has brought
into being" might not "lead to a very important shift in accent in
magisterial pronouncements, without the church having to deny
any dogmas that it has already defined."[9] Here, in the face of a
church that is all too ready to moralize, a church that is always
falling back upon human guilt, Rahner very gently asks us to consider if there must not also be a place in the church's proclamation and spirituality for complaint and for an insistent
questioning of God on the part of human beings faced with the
horrors of God's creation. Here again there always remains an
uneasiness over the suffering of the innocent, and over sin in general.[10] At any rate, Rahner resists any attempt on the part of theology to reconcile itself with God behind the back of the history of
human suffering. He knows how such "reconciliations" have led
to the moral rebellion of human beings against God and have in
this way turned out to be one of the roots, perhaps *the* root of
modern atheism.

Rahner's struggle for the theological dignity of men and
women, his theological respect for their suffering, has still
another side. He also resists any attempt to get around human
suffering by grasping it as God's suffering and sharing of suffering. Despite the highly respectable attempts in contemporary
Catholic as well as Protestant theology—in Karl Barth and Eberhard Jüngel, in Dietrich Bonhoeffer and Jürgen Moltmann, and
in Rahner's Catholic colleague, Hans Urs von Balthasar—
nowhere has he joined in this discourse about the suffering God,
about suffering between God and God, about suffering in God.
He has explicitly emphasized that Christology neither requires
nor authorizes theology to talk about a suffering God. He
pointed out that the filial consciousness of the poor and suffering human Jesus of Nazareth with regard to his divine Father
cannot be understood in the same sense as statements about the
inner-divinely, eternally begotten Son. He insisted on respect for

the nontransferable negative mystery of human suffering, which humankind may not begrudge God, for the sake of God and for the sake of humankind. "To put it very primitively—it does not help me at all to get out of my dirty mess and my despair just because things are going just as badly for God."[11]

How, in other words, is discourse about the suffering God not finally just a sublime duplication of human suffering and human powerlessness, or discourse that neutralizes the negativity of human suffering? Is it really only by chance that theology is talking, in an almost euphoric way, about a God who suffers and shares suffering, precisely at a time when aesthetics and aestheticization have taken on a key role in our postmodern sort of worldview? Putting the question differently (and in a way that I think follows Rahner's own intention), does not all this talk of the suffering God reveal something like an aestheticization of all suffering? Today in theology a great deal is being made of the love of God by which God shares in suffering. And in all of this it is taken for granted that this suffering love is invincible. But what kind of suffering is it that ultimately cannot lose anything, that cannot founder, that does not face the threat of total collapse? In the above-mentioned short essay, Rahner continually reminds us not to underestimate the negativity of human suffering. After all, suffering is at root something quite different from a strong, solidaristic sharing of suffering. It is nothing great and exalted. Neither is it simply a sign and expression of love, but rather much more a frightening symptom that one is no longer able to love. Suffering is reduced to nothingness if it is not a suffering unto God.

Suffering unto God: for me this is the key phrase that summarizes Rahner's theological existence, in which he became, for me and for many others, not only a teacher but also a father in faith. Rahner never interpreted Christianity as some sort of bourgeois domestic religion that has been purged of every hope threatened by death and purged of every vulnerable and stubborn longing. I never felt his understanding of faith to be a kind of security-ideology. There was always a homelessness; through

everything there remained a longing I never felt to be sentimental, nor Pollyannaishly optimistic. Here was not a longing that
would storm the heavens, but much more a hushed sigh of the
creature, like a wordless cry for light before the hidden face of
God.

7

The Church After Auschwitz

I. AUSCHWITZ—A SIGN OF THE TIMES?

Since the last council there has been a great deal of discussion in the Catholic Church about the so-called signs of the times that have to be understood in the light of faith and processed with the power of hope. But what would these signs of the times be? What marks the countenance of our century? What will people of the twenty-first century remember, if they still remember? What monuments, what time-signs of this saeculum of ours, coming to a close? It would be well worth a poll. Would "Auschwitz" be among them? I doubt it. Do ecclesial pronouncements on the signs of the times talk about Auschwitz? Not to my knowledge. The title of this essay recognizes Auschwitz, recognizes the Shoah, as such a time-sign for the church, the church after Auschwitz. This obviously rather untimely sign of the times should be the topic of discussion here, so the comment Elie Wiesel has made (not in a denunciatory tone, but more with a note of sadness) will not be true of the ecclesial lives of Christians: "Yesterday it went: Auschwitz? Never heard of it. Today: Auschwitz. Oh yes, I already know about that." Do we really know about it? Do we know what happened as a result of Auschwitz, what happened to us, to our Spirit of Christianity and our often so forgetful, so clever talk about God and the world? From Elie Wiesel comes a statement that sounds awful to Christian ears: "The thoughtful Christian knows that it was not the Jewish people that died in Auschwitz, but rather Christianity." We can only stand firm before this pronouncement if we do not simply ignore the experiences that prompted it.

II. AFTER AUSCHWITZ

What does it mean to grasp and characterize our situation as a situation after Auschwitz?

There is Theodore Adorno's dictum that "after Auschwitz there can no longer be any poetry." Who still dares cite this saying today without irony or without a shrug of the shoulders? For has not the course of time long ago proven it false? Was it not really wide of the mark? Does not this saying sound as if, after Auschwitz, birds would be forbidden to sing, the flowers to bloom, the sun to shine? Yet what is it that distinguishes human beings from birds, flowers and the sun? Is it not the terror, dismay over the revelation that occurred in Auschwitz at the inhumanity of human beings? Is it not the horror striking them dumb, interrupting their singing, making the sun go dark? Are we human beings really more humane when we are able successfully to forget such a horrible fact about ourselves?

What does *after Auschwitz* mean for the church? Where Auschwitz is concerned one can hardly be too radical, but can very easily be too ingenious or too *original*. And so it must not be too much on our minds, even (especially) among theologians. When it comes to the church and to being a Christian after Auschwitz, one thing occurs to me above all; I have often repeated it through the years, and ask your indulgence if I begin here by talking about it again. It concerns the memory of a conversation from the sixties. At that time a panel discussion was held in Münster between the Czech philosopher Milan Machovec, Karl Rahner, and myself. Toward the end of the discussion Machovec reminded me of that saying of Adorno—"After Auschwitz there can no longer be any poetry."—and asked me whether after Auschwitz there could be any prayer anymore for us Christians. I responded in the same way I would today: We can pray after Auschwitz because even in Auschwitz there were prayers—in the songs and in the cries of the Jewish victims. To be sure, not every victim was a Jew, but every Jew was one of the victims. Being a Jew meant per se being condemned to death, per se being excluded from the community of human beings. Thus Auschwitz stands for the Jewish fate in the Western and European world, in the Christian world.

We Christians will never return to a time before Auschwitz; we will never get beyond Auschwitz alone, but only together with the victims of Auschwitz. In my view, this is what it will cost if Christianity is to continue on the other side of Auschwitz. Do not say: But after all, there are for us Christians experiences of God other than those of Auschwitz. Certainly! However, if there is no God for us in Auschwitz, how can there be a God for us anywhere else? And do not say: Such a notion violates the heart of the Christian teachings that tell us how in Jesus Christ the nearness of God is irrevocably guaranteed to Christians. Because the question remains: For which Christianity is this promise valid? For example, does it hold for a Christianity that identifies itself with anti-Semitism and is among the historical roots of Auschwitz? or does it hold exclusively for a Christianity that can only understand and proclaim its own identity in the face of this history of Jewish suffering? For me the recognition of this (as it were) salvation-historical dependency is the test of whether we are prepared as Christians to grasp the catastrophe of Auschwitz precisely as such, whether we are ready to do more than merely exorcise it ethically, as is commonly done, and instead take it seriously both ecclesially and theologically.

Can our horror be trusted, our confession of guilt, our shame that we have lived and prayed with our backs to Auschwitz? Can our dismay be trusted, our horror over our secret or even open complicity with the murderous persecution of the Jews carried out by the Nazis, horror at the indifference with which we Germans thrust the Jews, along with those few of us who stood with them, into deadly isolation? Can one trust that Christian theology has finally learned its lesson, that it is on guard against that veiled anti-Semitism that indeed hardly ever emerges in theology in the

form of a crude racism, but rather in metaphysical or psychological garb? Is it on its guard against an anti-Semitism that has accompanied Christian theology as a constitutional temptation from its
very beginnings, since the time of Marcion and since the irruption
of Gnosticism? Has the memory of Auschwitz transformed us in
our existence as Christians? Are we in fact a church after
Auschwitz? Or are we as Christians, as a church, the same as we
were yesterday? As Christian theologians do we speak the same way
today we spoke yesterday, before Auschwitz?

III. GOD AFTER AUSCHWITZ

The small town in the Upper Palatinate where I was born
belongs to the Archdiocese of Bamberg. In Bamberg Cathedral,
where I was ordained, there is, besides other famous works of art,
the symbolically rich pair of women representing Church and Synagogue. And just as in Strasbourg Cathedral, in Bamberg the synagogue is depicted as a woman with blindfolded eyes.

When I look upon this image of the synagogue with blindfolded eyes today I am deeply troubled by the question of what
her eyes have seen, what they know of God, and what we in
Christendom—frequently with extreme violence—have theologically made invisible and silenced. For instance, when I see this
image today I ask myself whether during that night when the syn-
agogues burned in Germany a wisdom about God was reduced
to ashes, a wisdom without which today we Christians cannot
know our own hearts or minds when we say "God," nor when we
say "Jesus" (who, as everyone knows, was not a Christian but
rather a Jew). Reflecting on the figure of this woman today, I see
it as a symbol and monumental memory of the biblical Israel,
and then ask myself, as a Christian and a member of my church,
how I must understand and value Israel's election by God, by the
one God of Jews and Christians. I ask myself how I must understand and value the unfinished covenant between God and "his"
people. What is it then (so I have often asked myself, in complete
accord with Paul) that makes even us Christians see Israel as

unsurpassable and irreplaceable? What is it that allows us to see the finger of God over this people? What really distinguishes biblical Israel? What distinguishes this small, culturally rather unremarkable and politically insignificant desert people from the glittering high cultures of its time, from Egypt, Persia or Greece? Israel knew no mythical or ideational riches in spirit with which it could transcend or console itself when it faced its own fears, the alienation of its exile, the history of suffering continually breaking out in its midst. It remained, in its inmost essence, mythically and idealistically mute. It showed little gift for forgetting, and at the same time little gift for the automatic, idealistic handling of disillusionment, and little gift for soothing its anxieties. It remained poor in spirit.

Even when, infiltrated by foreign cultures, Israel imported and mimicked myths and idealizing conceptions, it nonetheless was never completely and finally consoled by them. I could almost say that Israel's election, its capacity for God, showed itself in this particular incapacity, that is, the incapacity to let itself be really consoled by ahistorical myths or ideas. Compared with the glittering high cultures of its time—in Egypt, Persia and Greece—Israel remained in the final analysis an eschatological landscape of cries, a landscape of expectation as did, incidentally, early Christianity. The latter's biography, as everyone knows, ends with a cry (Rv 22:20), a cry now christologically intensified, a cry we have since then virtually reduced to silence, either mythically or idealistically-hermeneutically. Yet even over Christianity there lies a trace of something unreconciled. Even Christians' Christology is not without eschatological uneasiness. Not vaguely wandering questions, but passionate and insistent interrogation belongs to that passion for God that Christians—according to Paul—must come to terms with in the Jewish traditions.

Could it be that there is too much singing and not enough crying out in our Christianity? Too much jubilation and too little mourning, too much approval and too little sense for what is absent, too much comfort and too little hunger for consolation? In its moral teachings, is the church not too often on the side of Job's friends and too little on the side of Job himself, who thought faith could include even insistently questioning God? Do we believe in God—or do we believe in our faith in God, and therein in our selves, or in what we would like to hold about ourselves? If however we believe in God, can we remove from that faith the elements of crying out and expectation? Here one of the constitutional temptations of Christianity is rooted. I am reminded of Jesus' cry from the cross. From the very beginning the Christian community has found it difficult to deal with the fact that at the center of Christian faith there is that cry of the Son, abandoned by God. The history of the tradition shows how the shock this cry occasions was later attenuated, and the cry replaced by more pious farewells: in Luke, for example, by the words from the evening prayer of Psalm 31:6, "Into your hands I commend my spirit" or in John, by "It is finished." Only in the Letter to the Hebrews (5:7) is the great cry with which Jesus died again recalled (as J. Moltmann does).

This is true even for Christians: Whoever hears the message of the resurrection of Christ in such a way that in it the cry of the crucified has become inaudible, hears not the Gospel but a myth of the victors.

Elie Wiesel reported of his reencounter with Auschwitz in 1987 that "on the walk to the place where the slaves had built their gas chambers and crematoria it was necessary to clamp one's teeth. And every wish to wail, to cry out, to weep, had to be suppressed. At one point, at which we were in the antechamber of death, we who had been here once before felt the need to reach out to each other. The need to support one another? For an endless stretch of time we kept very still. Then, very quietly at first, but finally crying out louder and louder, like madmen we began to speak that eternal prayer of the Jews: Shema Israel—"Hear oh Israel, God is our God, God is one"—once, twice, five times. Did we do this because the victims, who sensed that the end was near, began to speak the same prayer? Because, in the end, on the threshold of death, all words turn into prayers, and all prayers come down to that one?"

Obviously religion is a primordial phenomenon of humanity;

the history of humanity has always been also the history of religion. In the *Shema Israel*, for the first time and in a unique way in the religious history of humanity, the name *God* was laid upon human beings. What later comes to be named biblical monotheism is rooted in Israel's passion for God—in the dual sense of a passion for God and as a suffering unto God. This monotheism is not, as its despisers like to caricature it, a totalitarian ideology of domination. It is, if I understand it aright, much more a pathic monotheism, with a painfully open eschatological flank, than it is a monotheism of power politics. I ask myself, again and again, How is it that what Jesus prophesied of himself can be more clearly discerned in the fate of Judaism after Christ than it can be in the destiny of Christianity itself?

As long as we are only talking about religion, as that is understood in our mythically enthralled, proreligious postmodern world, one can certainly dispense with Israel and the Jewish traditions. But if it is God and prayer that are at stake, then Israel is indispensable, not only for the Jews but also for us Christians. Israel, rejected and persecuted, is and continues to be the root for us Christians, and also for Islam. And thus Auschwitz is and continues to be an attack on everything that must be holy to us.

IV. AUSCHWITZ AND GERMANY

Auschwitz must not be functionalized; it must not be instrumentalized—not religiously, and not politically. I would agree with the Jewish historian Wolfsohn in this: since Germany was not geographically divided on account of Auschwitz, but rather because of power politics and ideological motives, it need not continue to be divided on account of Auschwitz. Pressing questions arise, of course, given our rewon unity. Now that what belongs together has come back together, will the wound that bears the name of Auschwitz be opened? With the passing of the so-called postwar period, will we also bury the memory of Auschwitz? Is there not the danger that with our unification we will return to an allegedly seamless normality and continuity in our German history? But that would not be a unity built on a responsible awareness of history! It would only stir up new fears, and not exclusively for the Jews among us, though in a very particular way for them.

Do we have enough sensitivity and respect for new fears arising among the Jews in our midst, the few who were able to save themselves and have risked remaining among us or returning to us? For a church that wants to understand itself as a church after Auschwitz, a new arena is opening up in which the church must prove itself. It is precisely the church that must insist that our newly won unity not forget the horrified faces of our Jewish fellow citizens. It must insist that we cannot encourage any understanding of German unity that overlooks anew, or even secretly excludes, our elder brothers and sisters in faith, as John Paul II calls the Jews. This is what Christians among the Auschwitz-generation must pass on to the next generation.

It may be that everything comes down to this: It is precisely because of unification that we are confronted once again with our recent history, that we will all together be drawn anew into history, a postwar history in which the memory of Auschwitz was too often repressed in the West, while in the East it was, at best, ideologically functionalized. This recapitulation harbors an opportunity, but also a growing danger against which we must be on our guard. For it is precisely repetitions, lags in political history, that can quickly lead us astray into *ressentiment,* into zealously sharpened attitudes; they easily promote aggressiveness and latent violence. So we must not be in any way indifferent to a rising anti-Semitism or, more generally, to a growing xenophobia among us. German unity must never gather beneath these banners. Such signs of the times would have to be particularly resisted by the church in Germany, from their very beginning and without compromise, if it is to understand itself as a church after Auschwitz. Such a stance does not preclude critical questions for the contemporary State of Israel; a wholesale suspension of critique would be here more a withdrawal from solidarity, containing (as do so many varieties of vague philo-Semitism) once again the germ of new anti-Semitic thinking. Two points seem important to me for a German critique of political Israel:

1. No German critique of the State of Israel must be made unless such criticism is present in Israel itself.

2. It is precisely as Germans that we should be the last to object to an exaggerated need for security and preservation among the Jews, given the fact they were brought to the verge of annihilation in our recent history. And we should be first in giving them the benefit of a doubt when they assert that they defend their state not out of Zionist imperialism, but rather as a shelter against death, as the final refuge for a people that has been persecuted down through the centuries.

V. AUSCHWITZ AND EUROPE

Over the past year German television ran a four-part series by journalist Lea Rosh on the fate of the Jews in Europe under Nazi rule, with commentary by the historian Eberhard Jaekel. The final line in the last installment was "Europe—a cemetery for the Jews." Those concluding words were not meant to deflect German guilt for the mass-murder of millions of Jews, which is what the name Auschwitz stands for. After all, the whole series appeared under a title borrowed from Paul Celan: *Death is a* Meister *from Germany*. Nor did it intend to throw doubt on what the series itself documented: that in many of the countries allied with or occupied by Germany, especially in Italy, there was highly courageous resistance against this tidal wave of annihilation.

"Europe—a cemetery for the Jews." Can we come to terms with such words at a time when Europe has once again become the focus of our interest? I will try to discuss that question from the perspective of a church after Auschwitz.

In a rather abbreviated fashion it may be said that what we today call Europe, as we have come to know it from its 2000-year history, was shaped by the Greek spirit on the one hand and Christianity on the other. The Jewish spirit, so it would seem, does not belong to this definition of Europe, and has no right to

reside *[Heimatrecht]* there.[1] The emancipation of the Jews carried
on since the Enlightenment was only supposed to be possible
under the presupposition of their emancipation from the Jewish
spirit. Johann Gottlieb Fichte, exponent of a German Idealism
that influenced and defined not only the German spirit but the
European spirit, said it thus: "They [the Jews] must have human
rights…but I see no other way of granting them civil rights than
this: one night all their heads have to be removed and replaced
with others that contain not even one Jewish idea."[2]

Here is where my question arises for Christianity and for the
church. Should not the Jewish spirit, together with the Christian
spirit, have been propagated in Europe by the Christians? If for
no other reason than the fact that Jesus was a Jew, and that his
disciples were Jews? Very early on, a problematic and momen-
tous strategy for spiritually disinheriting Israel set in, both eccle-
siologically and theologically. (1) The church understood itself
too exclusively as the new Jerusalem, as the authentic people of
God. The foundational significance of Israel for Christians, as
Paul so emphatically urged it in his Letter to the Romans, was
too quickly suppressed; the root of Jesse was reduced to a now-
surpassed presupposition within the church's salvation history.
(2) Very early on something I call the bisection of the spirit of
Christianity set in in theology: one could certainly appeal to
Israel's faith tradition, but the spirit *[Geist]* is drawn exclusively
from Athens, from the Greek-Hellenistic traditions. Had Israel
and the Jewish-biblical traditions, then, no spirit to offer to
Christianity and therefore to the European spirit as well? But
there is such a Jewish spirit, offered to the spirit of Christianity
and to the European spirit; and only when this Jewish spirit has
the right to reside *[Heimatrecht]* within the European spirit will
the synagogue as well be not merely endured, but recognized
and appreciated.

I would describe the Jewish spirit as the power of memory, a
power unknown or continually repressed in Europe. Jewish memory resists forgetfulness, even the forgetfulness of the forgotten. In
the final analsyis, for it, wisdom is a form of sensing absence. It

does not resist just the forgetfulness that wants to wipe away every trace, so that finally nothing can be remembered (as, for example, the Nazis tried to do with the demolition of the death-chambers). It does not resist just this intentional suppression, but as well even the forgetfulness that lies hidden in every pure historicization of the past. Such remembering is not only a matter of individual ethics, nor a matter for science alone; it is a concern for culture, the expression of an anamnestic culture that is at home in Judaism. This Jewish culture of remembering is lacking both in European Christianity and in the European spirit as a whole.

Are we European Christians blind to the dignity of this anamnestic culture? Have we already placed ourselves too far beyond it and cast it off as archaic or premodern? Yet it is true also for the faith of Christians that it not only *has* a remembrance, but *is* a remembrance: the memory of the suffering, the death and the resurrection of Jesus Christ. We Christians have certainly preserved this remembrance-structure of our faith in our cult ("Do this in remembrance of me."). But have we cultivated it enough also in the public sphere? Have we formed it and defended it in the intellectual and cultural spheres? Or have we not in those places continued to be latter-day Platonists?

And have we forgotten that Christianity is not only deeply indebted to the Greek spirit, but has also again and again foundered against it? We know of this foundering from the earliest history of the church in Christianity, from the Acts of the Apostles, where it tells of Paul on the Areopagus in Athens. Paul was certainly able to find common ground with the Greeks there concerning an "unknown god." However, when he spoke to them of what ties us absolutely to the Jewish traditions, when he spoke to them of eschatology and apocalypticism, of the God who raises the dead, then it says "some scoffed; but others said, 'We will hear you again about this.' At that point Paul left them" (Acts 17: 32f.). The spirit of remembering that is at work in the biblical stories of hope cannot simply be sublated *[aufgehoben]* into the Greek spirit. But who then has saved and preserved this spirit of remembering—for Christianity, for Europe?

Are we not totally lacking the Jewish culture of remembering here in Europe? Is not the modern European person less and less his or her own remembrance, and more and more only his or her own experiment? Are we thereby to conclude that authentic progress is the progressive loss of remembering? The recent dispute among historians over the evaluation of Auschwitz always aroused in me the question whether we were dealing with this catastrophe in such an uncertain and divisive way because we lacked the spirit which was supposed to have been definitively extinguished in Auschwitz, if it was not because we lack the spirit of memory which would be needed to perceive what had happened in a catastrophe of this sort, even to us, to Europe, and finally to us Christians?

On the eighth of May 1990, participants in the Jewish World Congress gathered in front of the so-called Wannsee villa in Berlin, in order to commemorate the liberation from Nazi rule forty-five years earlier. At that meeting a text by Elie Wiesel read in Hebrew, German and English recalled the plan for annihilation conceived in Wannsee. Here is the final passage: "But Wannsee also means for us Jews that memory is stronger than its foes. It means that the hope of the Jews has triumphed over their fear. It means that coming back to Wannsee and listening to the hard, dark echoes of those voices, we Jews want to save coming generations from having our past become their inheritance for the future." This is the Jewish dowry for Europe, for humanity, for a church after Auschwitz.

8

Theology and the University

Today universities are universities without universalism and without universalists. Nothing comes across as more suspicious than the universal, and so theologians are probably the last universalists left in the university. For if one engages in theology—that is, attempts to speak about God—one is committed to universality. Either God is a universal theme for all humanity, or it is just no theme at all. But, it will be said, God is no longer to be found in the modern sciences *[Wissenschaften]*. Well and good. But is the human being to be found any more in our modern disciplines? Or have we not come to the point at which discourse about "man" has turned into the most glaring anthropomorphism of our scientific world—and that includes the increasingly subjectless, technomorphic systems-language of the humanities? Whoever does theology, whoever tries to speak about God, must also always speak about a human being who is not only his own experiment, but—more fundamentally—his own memory, who is recognizable not only by means of his structures and functions, but also by means of his histories. It may well be that this position can only be advocated in the ensemble of today's academic disciplines with a goodly portion of metaphysical civil courage. If so, then that is precisely what we need.

THE AUTHORITY OF THOSE WHO SUFFER

Presumably we also need civil courage in view of another universalism, which I would also like to mention, since I hold it to be

133

indispensable even today, in these times of postmodern sensitivity to the undeniable dangers in all universalistic orientations. I am thinking of the universalism of responsibility, in the face of the much-bemoaned moral bankruptcy of Europe, in the face of exaggerated individualization and the diffusion of our life-worlds, which appear no longer to be structured by any binding remembrance. The traditions to which theology is accountable know a universal responsibility born of the memory of suffering. This *memoria passionis* becomes the basis of a universal morality by the fact that it always takes into account the suffering of others, the suffering of strangers. Furthermore, this *memoria,* speaking quite biblically, considers even the suffering of enemies and does not forget about their suffering in assessing its own history of suffering. In such a way, to give an example, Rabin and Arafat began their peace process, which has become so fragile in the meantime: with the assurance that each would look not only at his own history of suffering, but also fix his eyes on the suffering of his former enemies. That is exemplary for a universal morality. It does not arise on the basis of a so-called minimal consensus, but rather when the need arises on the basis of a continually renewed fundamental consensus between peoples and cultures. In my view there is one authority recognized by all great cultures and religions: the authority of those who suffer. Respecting the suffering of strangers is a precondition for every culture; articulating others' suffering is the presupposition of all claims to truth. Even those made by theology.

To be sure, Christianity is not primarily a moral system, but a hope; its theology is not primarily an ethics, but an eschatology. But precisely therein lie the roots of its ability not to surrender or diminish its measure of responsibility, even in the face of alleged or actual powerlessness. The sole content of its universal responsibility is this: There is no suffering in the world that does not concern us.[1] This proposition need not be understood as expressing a theological fantasy of omnipotence, but rather simply as the moral application of the proposition that all persons are equal; that is, it is the moral application of a proposition that is guaranteed not only through the biblical traditions, but also by the basic laws of modern constitutional states. Whether or not this universalism, at least in its outlines, succeeds ever and anew among us will ultimately decide whether Europe will be a glittering or a burning multicultural landscape, whether it will be a landscape of peace or of escalating civil wars. This universalism must not remain outside the gates of the *universitas.*

9

Monotheism and Democracy: Religion and Politics on Modernity's Ground

I. THE ISSUE

Religion will be understood here in the form that makes the relationship between religion and politics on modernity's ground a precarious one: that is to say, as the Christian religion whose monotheistic core has not yet been completely dissolved. Typical theories of modernity have relegated this religion to an anachronistic, or at any rate strictly private counterworld. They have denied it any potential for interpreting the relationship between religion and politics in a critical-productive way, and for accompanying and protecting the politics of modernity—in a stage of critical reflexivity and in the midst of upheavals in the logic for legitimating political action. How amenable is a monotheistic religion to modernity anyway? How amenable is modernity to monotheism?

Modernity has subjected monotheism to the sharpest political critique. For the most part monotheism has been considered to be the source of legitimation for a predemocratic, monarchical mentality, opposed to any sort of division of powers. It is seen as the root of an obsolete patriarchalism, and as inspiration for political fundamentalisms. We definitely must revisit this issue—especially since the relationship between religion and politics at the limits of modernity cannot be discussed only in terms of the tensions between Christianity and modernity. Rather, it is increasingly necessary that the discussion include the relationships of the other monotheistic religions to modernity: the root monotheistic religion of Judaism, and also that of Islam, with its pointed cultural conflicts with European modernity.

Politics will be understood here as liberal politics in constitutional democracies, as it becomes reflexive. This is intended to imply the following: the liberal substance of politics has now lost the *negative warrant* provided by totalitarian systems, and finds heretofore assumed *ligatures* breaking down, prereflexive reserves of tradition and milieu and of cultural coherence.[1] Thus politics, which for its part considers itself modernity's favorite child, is required to justify itself precisely on this modern ground. But what politics discovers at this stage of self-reflection is—crudely put—its groundlessness on modern ground. There is no stable center, no core for its self-reflection. What it views as its foundations are consensus, which can be revoked; the contract, which can be dissolved or certainly renegotiated at any point; the institution, as a codification of social agreements that is in principle mutable, and so on. A high degree of uncertainty and insecurity are irrupting into that politics in its reflexive stage. In my view, this is the deeper source of the much-bemoaned apoliticality or political listlessness in democratic politics on the one hand, as well as of fundamentalist and populist reactions on the other.

How are we to deal with this? Can an enlightenment concerning the relationship of religion and politics on modernity's ground contribute something productive? Or has everything already been said and decided on the issue, so that any attempt at a new definition of the relationship must lead directly to dangerous reductions, to the quasifundamentalist erasure of differentiations in the relationship and to doomsday speculations about modernity in general? "All the possibilities of Christian life, the most serious and the most trivial, the most harmless and thoughtless, as well as the most reflective, have been thoroughly tried out; it is time to uncover something new, or else we will keep on running in the same old circles…"[2]

II. RELIGIOUS OR ARELIGIOUS SYMBOLIZATION OF POLITICAL LEGITIMACY IN MODERNITY?

Politics on modern ground: in the current view this means a politics without any anchoring in transcendence; a politics with a purely worldly legitimation of political rule; a politics strictly separated from religion and from all religious symbolizations of political legitimacy, or even those that are analogous to the religious. Is this, must this be the only way, if one would not fall back into premodern political models? Anyone who cautiously questions the irreversibility of these modernization processes, who wonders—guardedly—whether the radical privatization of religion is in every respect a good thing for the modern politics of freedom, must be very careful that in so doing she or he does not succumb to antiliberal, fundamentalistic traps. But are we already antidemocratic fundamentalists or antipluralist traditionalists, just because we do not want to judge the legitimacy of a political decision exclusively by the procedural correctness of the way it was made? If, for example, we ask how one could evaluate political events in Algeria using criteria drawn from a purely procedurally oriented, strictly formal rationality? If, in other words, we inquire not only about those rules at play in a functioning democracy that can be represented in discourse theory, but also about the resources for defending it?

I would like now to survey contemporary political theories in somewhat more detail. We find that, in all attempts to separate religion and politics in modernity, a strictly areligious codification of precisely this modern politics is hardly ever attained or sustained. It is certainly true in two recent German political and social theories. On one hand there are the recent, post-Marxist Frankfurters, and especially the penetrating thought of Helmut Dubiel. For him democracy is, "as it were, the institutionalized way of dealing in the public sphere with uncertainty." Is this accurate, or is it not—despite all the intricacy and depth of the argumentation—really too much the politics of the graduate seminar, with a touch of discourse aesthetics? At any rate, even

Dubiel risks a connection to religious symbolization, giving a typi-
cal-enough definition of "democracy as posttraditional 'civil religion.'"[3] On the other hand, we have advocates of so-called risky
freedoms, theoreticians of the society of risk, with its escalating
processes of individualization.[4] Of course their concept of politics
does not lead into discourse, but rather into a kind of existential-
political decisionism, which is also favored in certain forms of
recent political thought in Italy: for example, by the Hannah
Arendt scholar, Paolo Flores d'Arcais.[5]

Turning to Hannah Arendt: she has come to be seen as the theorist of politics strictly separated from religion on modernity's
ground, who finds in modern revolutions a completely new secu-
lar grounding for political action that is distinct from all premodern forms of politics and their sources of legitimation.[6] But then
is it only out of inconsistency (as Dubiel, for example, assumes)
that, when Hannah Arendt in her book on revolution takes up
the issue of how legitimation crises are to be dealt with, she falls
back once again on quasireligious symbolizations, that is, on a
quasicultic appeal to the history of the founding of the new politics? Or is she giving way after all to the typically Anglo-Saxon,
North American grounding of politics on modern grounds by
means of civil religion? In his well-known book *Democracy in America,* Alexis de Tocqueville writes the following about this way of
grounding politics:

> Despotism can get along without faith, but freedom cannot. Reli-
> gion is much more necessary to a republic than to a monarchy,
> and to democratic states more than any other. How could society
> escape catastrophe if the ethical bond is not strengthened whilst
> politics is dissolving it? And what is to be done with a people,
> which as its own lord, is not subservient to God?[7]

Ever since the influential work *Habits of the Heart,*[8] by Robert
Bellah (and his co-authors), these correlations have played an
important role in the American communitarianism debate, even
if the American concept of religion since its delineation by de
Tocqueville has lost considerably in substance, so that it is almost

impossible to see how that kind of religion can help at all anymore to preserve a modern politics of freedom from the destructive consequences of exaggerated individualism.[9] At any rate, the communitarianism debate, in all its (sometimes almost diametrically opposed) shades, demonstrates how difficult it is adequately to uncouple religion and politics. I cannot here go into the details of the debate as it has been carried on in recent years, nor into the concept of religion that has come to light in it. One important reason why the debate has already died out again among us is that the Anglo-Saxon and North American perspective on the relationship between religion and politics cannot simply be transferred to the Continental discussion. This is due to profound historical differences. The English and American Enlightenment was Protestant, it was nonconformist; it occurred among free churches and among believers. The Continental (French) Enlightenment was anticlerical, lay and atheistic.[10] This lay-atheistic trait of the Continental Enlightenment—as well as the corresponding understanding of revolution—must be seen in connection with a Catholicism committed to the *Ancien Régime.* Only with the Second Vatican Council did the Catholic Church declare itself also to be a religion of freedom, when in its "Decree on Religious Freedom" it started not with the abstract rights of the truth, but rather with the rights of the person in his or her truth. This short decree—which, by the way, was the only one of the conciliar documents whose initial draft was prepared by a North American theologian—engendered an unprecedented and protracted conflict in the postconciliar church. This conflict was connected to a growing cultural conflict within Catholicism itself, a conflict which to this day remains foreign to the Anglo-Saxon and North American democratic traditions and their understanding of religion.

In Agnes Heller's *Politik nach dem Tod Gottes* ["Politics After the Death of God"], politics on modernity's ground nonetheless preserves a formal sphere of theological history. Under the rubric of Jacques Derrida's "weak Messianism" she formulates that politics in this way:

An empty seat awaits the Messiah. If anyone does occupy it, we can be sure we would have then a perverse or hypocritical Messiah. If someone gets rid of the podium, that is the beginning of the end, for the spirit will abandon the community. Politics cannot make use of an empty podium; yet as long as the podium is left where it is, exactly in the middle of the room, fixed in its cautionary and perhaps even pathetic emptiness, then the politicians will always take its existence into account. Or at least they are free to take its existence into account. Everything else is pragmatism.[11]

For me this is reminiscent of recent philosophies in France—of Claude Lefort, Marcel Gauchet and others, with their characteristic talk about the "empty site of power," about an "empty site of the sacred," which according to Lefort is the condition for modern society being able to portray itself as an autonomous society.[12]

On the German scene, liberal political philosophy continues to be troubled by the so-called Böckenförde Paradox.[13] According to Ernst Wolfgang Böckenförde, the modern liberal state lives off presuppositions it can neither produce nor guarantee on its own, and which it therefore uses up without being able to replenish. This metapolitical paradox draws our attention once again to the abstract character of a liberal separation of religion and politics on modernity's ground. Of course many would find in this a theoretical affinity with the dangerous political theology of Carl Schmitt, a proximity from which the paradox itself allegedly derives. But could not the critique formulated in that paradox, which is a critique of the abstract separation of religion and politics on modernity's ground, be interpreted and justified instead within the framework of the new political theology that I have advocated? It starts from the fact that a critical questioning of the liberal separation of religion and politics need by no means end in hostility to the Enlightenment and to democracy— as it did with Carl Schmitt and his sources, as it did with Donoso Cortes and with the French traditionalists. It starts from the fact that a critical rapprochement between religion and politics on modernity's ground in no way leads necessarily to a decisionist theory of the state, or to the denial of every justification by political reason of political thought and action.

To give an extremely abbreviated justification of the new political theology's perspective, I refer to Kant's famous definition of Enlightenment, according to which one is enlightened when one "makes a public use of one's reason in all things."[14] To be sure, this classic definition of Enlightenment stands today in great need of clarification—just as much regarding *publicness* as regarding *reason*.[15] Who today can go on talking about reason, the one and universal reason? Distinctions and nuances regarding reason have become indispensable. Jürgen Habermas, for example, has had a great deal of influence on political theory because of the way he has succeeded in doing this with his concept of communicative reason. Of course, as far as a theory of democracy goes, his theory leads in my view to the so-called discourse concept, and consequently to the "dark shadow of proceduralism." However much I admire the communicative theory of action, the political theologian in me wants to get rid of this dark shadow. That is why I continue to advocate a broadening of the connotations of the concept of reason in the direction of an anamnestic reason endowed with the power of memory—in the direction of a reciprocal, but irreversible priority between anamnestic and communicative reason.[16]

The Enlightenment has never overcome a deeply rooted prejudice in the model of reason that it developed: the prejudice against memory. The Enlightenment promotes discourse and consensus, but—in its abstract, totalizing critique of traditions—underestimates the intelligible and critical power of memory. In my view we can only reckon with the insights of the dialectic of Enlightenment—for the most part once again forgotten or repressed—in the light that is shed by anamnestic reason. Only in that light can the Enlightenment enlighten itself about the disaster it has brought about; only in that light can it arrive at some understanding of the moral and political exhaustion of the Enlightenment, or, that is to say, of European modernity. Anamnestic reason is quite amenable to the Enlightenment and modernity; it gains its own legitimate universalism because it allows itself to be guided by a specific memory: the *memoria passionis,* that is, the memory of suffering, or more precisely the memory of someone else's suffering. Anamnestic reason, therefore, is not primarily led by an a priori of communication and agreement, but by an a priori of suffering. This a priori of suffering orients political discourse in times of uncertainty. It becomes the criterion of a liberal politics in those cases where the purely procedural point of view does not suffice for arriving at a political decision—especially in legitimation crises for political authority. How else can a free democracy protect itself from a political fundamentalism that comes to power in a procedurally correct fashion?

The political power of the memory of suffering is clearly evident in current areas of political conflict. In the former Yugoslavia, the purely self-referential memory of suffering in particular ethnic groups is leading to one orgy of violence after another. The rapprochement between Palestine and Israel, on the other hand, began with the mutual assurance by Rabin and Arafat that each would bear in mind not only his own suffering, but also the suffering of his former enemies. As fragile as this approach may be, given the realities of politics, who knows of a better or more promising one?

III. TWO ILLUSTRATIONS FOR CLARIFYING THE RELATIONSHIP BETWEEN RELIGION AND POLITICS ON MODERN GROUND

Religion and politics on modernity's ground: the attempt to offer a new definition will engender a plethora of questions and problems. Two of these, in no way arbitrarily selected, will be mentioned at least briefly here: the problem of universalism, and the question of traditions and institutions on modernity's ground.

1. We must look with special care at an understanding of monotheism that, in our view, has been subjected to sharpest critique because it is considered a clear example of incompatibility

with modernity. Monotheism based on the biblical passion for God, however, has nothing at all to do with the political monotheism that was justified, as Erik Peterson found, in a Graeco-Hellenic mirroring of the one God in the one rule *[mon-arché]*.[17] Evading such a monotheism of power politics does not at all require, in my view, the Christian dissolution of the monotheistic principle into trinitarian theology (as Peterson suggested). For authentic biblical monotheism is really a pathic monotheism, a monotheism that has a side sensitive to suffering, a monotheism constitutionally broken by the theodicy question, a question that can as little be answered as it can be forgotten. It is a monotheism for which history is not simply the history of the victors, but above all a history of suffering; a monotheism that is historically condensed in the biblical *memoria passionis* and can be universalized only through the remembrance of someone else's suffering, the suffering of others—up to and including even the suffering of one's enemies.[18] The question we must deal with here, therefore, is whether or not *this* monotheism can be combined with the conditions of modern political life. The struggle for this monotheism in the background of European modernity probably is of decisive significance for the looming cultural conflict between the political culture of the West and that of Islam, always presupposing that one does not represent this conflict too one-sidedly in favor of the West.

The liberal traditions, which start from a strict separation of religion and politics on modernity's ground, are naturally also aware of a political universalism: the universalism of the politics of human rights. In this case we are dealing with a procedural universalism, of course, a universalism of the rules of the game that are supposed to ensure agreement among persons and within humanity. My question is this: Is there no normative given for this agreement? Is it, to say it very plainly, guided by no authority whatsoever? There is, after all, one authority that has not been superseded by any of the critiques of authority formulated on modernity's ground: the authority of those who suffer. In my view every liberal politics aiming at the universal must reckon with this authority. Respecting someone else's suffering is a requirement for any political culture. And articulating others' suffering is the presupposition of all universalist claims, as they are formulated in the politics of human rights.[19] Only thus can there be forms of political action, new forms of solidarity, that have a universal orientation but do not become totalitarian. For the remembrance *[Eingedenken]* of someone else's suffering is by nature no passive observation; against its horizon resistance to suffering is unconditionally commanded, a resistance that is not guided by the myth of complete freedom from suffering, of course, but rather has a sober recognition that there will always be situations that create suffering among men and women.[20]

"There is no suffering in the world that does not concern us."[21] Is this a religious or a political statement? Is it the expression of a typically religious fantasy of omnipotence, or does it have something to do with the fundamental principles of modern constitutional democracies? Really, it is nothing other than the moral application of the statement of the equality of all men and women. Consequently, it is not only a statement to which the monotheism I have portrayed here, with its universal memory of suffering, is committed; it is as well a statement that forms the basis of the fundamental laws of modern constitutional states. Neither are liberal democracies without this universalistic base. But who is there today to defend this founding premise of modern democracies, now that the basic tension between freedom and equality expressed in the statement is being converted more and more into the superficial tension between freedom and security?[22]

The new definition of the relationship between religion and politics on modern ground in no way excludes a grounding of the politics of human rights in juridical reason. In that grounding, of course, formal rationality will not be able to dispense with the support provided by anamnestic rationality. Anamnestic reason attains its rationality in the form of the remembrance of someone else's suffering, as the foundation of every universal political culture and of the cultural reserves of every liberal democracy. Although anamnestic reason is formed in part by the great monotheistic traditions, although it in this sense dates back to premodern origins, it is thoroughly capable of pluralism, and recommends itself to modernity's political discussion about human rights under the a priori of respect for the suffering of others.

I stress this so explicitly and at such length because a different version of political theology, by Carl Schmitt, is I believe once again gaining influence on the contemporary scene, and not just in Germany. Schmitt states, very succinctly, "Whoever says humanity, intends deception."[23] While my political theology starts from the universalism of suffering, without thereby being guided by the myth of freedom from suffering, Schmitt's political theology puts its money on the universalism of sin, particularly of original sin. This is not only the root of Schmitt's skepticism regarding the human capability for democratic self-rule, but also the starting-point for his fundamental political axiom of the friend-foe con-stellation, as well as for his notion of a society that is always latently caught up in civil war and consequently needs a powerful, decisionistic state to hold back this inherent danger. A portion of what used to be the left in Germany, including people like Hans Magnus Enzensberger, Botho Strauß and Karl-Heinz Bohrer, today has ended up being astonishingly close to Carl Schmitt. For them, the universalism in every ethic of human rights is the real "moral trap."[24] Civil war is in every respect seen as the pressing problem.

> Actually, civil war penetrated the metropolises a long time ago. Its metastases are a part of everyday life in the large cities.… Civil war is not coming from the outside; it is no foreign virus, but rather an indigenous process.[25]

And so it is the former left wing that today is clamoring for a strong, decisionist state. What is more, it seems like decisionism is being called for today on all sides: if not on the part of the state, then in the style of that existential-political decisionism propagated by our theoreticians of risky freedoms. As I see it, this new trend toward decisionistic ideas reflects the uncertainty and insecurity that presses in upon the liberal constitutional democracies in their self-reflective mode. Is democracy possible then only as permanently institutionalized discourse? Or are there still some other ways of responding democratically to a situation in which the justificatory logic of political action is breaking down?

2. From the standpoint of theories of modernity, the so-called premodern age is looked upon as the time of the foundation of monotheistic religion, whereas modernity is seen as the time when it was critiqued or critically hemmed in. Is this critique so exhaustive that it rules out any sort of traditionally oriented forms of justification? To put it differently, is a society in which the project of modernity has succeeded and matured in this sense necessarily and irreversibly a post-traditional society, as the contemporary Frankfurt School suggests? Are the political Enlightenment and modern politics made up exclusively of strictly, discursively filtered memories? Are there no longer any discourse-orienting traditions at all, traditions that could preserve discourse from its own formalism and substantive desertification? To be sure, one cannot reanimate dead or dried-up traditions by showing how necessary they really are, or by showing everything they could accomplish. But this is not my issue either. Rather, my question is this:

Are there any institutions left on our modern ground that conceive of themselves as their accumulated memories, as a depository of memories, available for the structuring of a diffuse and discursively unmanageable life-world? Are there any institutions left on our modern ground that can offset a way of dealing with traditions that has become reflexive among us, and thus bring to bear in politics the indispensability of traditions, an indispensability that for the most part we have only been able to formulate aporetically?[26] Are there institutions like this? And if there are, then do not religious institutions (among others, but not least among them) belong in that ensemble? Religious institutions, in other words, that harbor a freedom-saving core precisely because (to recall once again the monotheistic axiom) the *memoria passionis* they represent is presented by them as the memory of someone else's suffering? Admittedly, such a definition of the classical religious institution can hardly evade the suspicion of idealization. It can only be authenticated by the institution, for its part, subjecting itself again and again to the remembrance that has been built up in it; in short, by its becoming an *ecclesia semper reformanda.*

Allow me to say what I find enticing in this presumptuous conjecture about religious institutions on modernity's ground. The processes of extreme individualization in our society are drifting into sheer hopelessness. Who is responding to the new need to simplify our complex world, to give some relief in the midst of conditions that no one person can grasp any more, to provide structure in our diffuse life-worlds, to slow down a situation that is accelerating out of control, and so on? Who is responding to these needs with a structuring remembrance, one that protects the individual as much from imploding processes of individualization as from the grip of the Leviathan, the powerful state of a Carl Schmitt? What does the legitimate liberal principle mean anymore, the one formulated by R. Dahrendorf: "Freedom is not freedom from institutions, but freedom through institutions"?[27] For does the increasingly extreme process of individualization have anything but dysfunctional effects?

What is one to make of a recommendation like this one given by the risk theorist, Beck: "Individualization means detraditionalization, but also the contrary, the invention of traditions."[28] Has not the social-technical master-myth of the reproducibility of anything and everything—that is, even of life-giving traditions—long ago penetrated this suggestion to "invent" traditions? What does any of this have to do with freedom-preserving traditions and institutions anyway? How does one snatch individuals away from their political narcissism? How is one to understand an individual who refuses to attest to traditions that, for their part, attest to the individual? When all is said and done, does not the capacity for democracy and pluralism depend upon a prior remembrance that overcomes the self-referentiality of individuals through respect for the suffering of others, and thus becomes the foundation for varied political cultures and for the cultural reserves of a liberal democracy? Dubiel is of a decidedly different opinion:

At the end of the twentieth century...there no longer exists any ethical sphere *[Sittlichkeit]* that is defined by a tradition, in whose name one could once again provide boundaries for and to a modernity that has fallen into crisis....Consequently, advanced societies began some time ago to produce themselves the cultural conditions needed for their existence.[29]

Is it only embittered cultural pessimism, if I have the impression that the cultural conditions produced by advanced societies turn out to be little more than the logic of the market or of exchange? and that consequently an allegedly presuppositionless, purely formal rationality is in actual fact guided by a (hidden) a priori of the market, wherein the market rewards dispositions that make one ready to negotiate? Here it seems to me that the traditionally rooted a priori of suffering is still more promising—even and precisely for modernity's politics. Prior to every relationship of exchange and competition, it entails the metapolitical guarantee of a turn to the other. And it traces its origins, at least, to those traditions I have here described as pathic monotheism.

10

A Passion for God:
Religious Orders Today

Foreword

Why refer to religious orders with this passionate title? Do they not find themselves in the midst of a crisis that appears even more intractable today than it did when, in 1977, I placed a question mark—certainly with concern, but also with confidence—in the title of my book on this subject?[1] At that point, venturing forth from council and synod, it meant that the hour of discipleship was in a particular way the time of Christians in religious orders—not because they "are the exclusive representatives of following Christ, but because following Christ (which is something all Christians without question are called to do) needs an energetic stimulus; it demands to be lived in a radical way that can plainly be observed."[2]

With today's postmodern nonchalance, statements like this sound like an overworked message from times past. And it simply is not true that it has been first and foremost the religious who have given the message practical plausibility here in Europe. Rather, for their part, they seem to have pulled themselves together and have devoted themselves to their own vocation crisis: hope waxes or wanes with numbers. But such hope alone is not enough.

The conviction expressed in the earlier book on religious orders was that the crisis they faced was only secondarily a vocation crisis, but primarily one of function.[3] This is probably still true enough today that it can be applied again and in a more general way, since more is involved here than just religious life. If it is

150

true we are living in a cultural climate that pays homage to what is tantamount to proreligious Godlessness, then the question of the *vita religiosa* is more pressing than ever. Here I am thinking of a *vita* that secures more than the mere survival of Christianity in this still- or postmodern time, and thus is in even greater need of what *Followers of Christ* called "productive prototypes"—both within and outside the orders. For what is really at stake is a fundamental theme of Christianity: a passion for God that encompasses the suffering and passion of those who will not let themselves be dissuaded from God, even when the rest of the world already believes that religion does not need God anymore. In that sense, my query into the existence of religious orders involves a condensed portrait of radical Christian existence today.

The following text, "Religion, Yes—God, No", reproduces the essentials of a talk I gave in June 1990 in Würzburg to the Annual Meeting of the Assembly of Superiors of German Religious Orders, fourteen years after my lecture "A Time for the Orders?" was given in the same context. The theme proposed for the 1990 talk was "Signs of the Times—the Response of the Orders."

RELIGION, YES—GOD, NO

Christianity has been rendered radically problematic in this supposedly post-Christian age, and because of this the distinction between Christians in religious life and ordinary Christians really should be considered a secondary one. At most it means that the situation in which Christianity in general finds itself—if and to the extent that it is to be understood and assessed as something more than merely a cultural, aesthetic, or psychological phenomenon—can be readily seen in stark relief in the situation of religious communities.

I. When Things Get Dangerous

I will not spend too much time with the issue of legitimating on Christian grounds the separate existence of religious orders,

although we all know that this has been called into question ever
since the Reformation. In my little book, *Followers of Christ* (which,
indeed, goes back to a lecture I gave you in 1976), I began by trying
to sketch out the authentic meaning of religious life in the contemporary life of the church and of society.[4] To the degree that I am
competent to speak on these matters, not being a member of a religious order, I say today what I said then. With Kierkegaard, I am of
the opinion that Luther "struck too strongly" when he rejected the
separate existence of religious orders, of monasticism, giving up
that "interim-authority" (as Kierkegaard called it in this context)
that tries to make a case for the seriousness and radicality of Christianity in a bourgeois-tempered, still- or postmodern Christendom—not, to be sure, in magisterial robes, but rather with a vivid
and compelling form of life.[5]

A Christianity that has not outlived itself always needs men and
women who "are deranged by possibility," the possibility of God
in our world, a world wherein another madman—the madman in
Nietzsche's *Gay Science*—announced long ago the death of God.[6]
And a Christianity that has not completely historicized the situation and impulse of its founding, thus putting it behind itself,
needs ever anew men and women who still try to take some things
literally from the Word of God, and therefore refuse to stifle its
provocative and scandalous character by means of a purely psychological hermeneutic (to give one example), with its zeal for
normalcy.[7]

At its core, Christianity functions as a grand exaggeration that
from a purely psychological perspective may appear thoroughly
delusional. The standards for attentiveness, devotion and responsibility for the other which Jesus mapped out are disturbing, scandalous. An air of anarchy hovers over his message. Who can live
this message consistently? Thus for two thousand years we have
labored to diminish these standards, to prune them back, so we
can manage them without having to risk too much conversion.
Yet again and again in Christianity, alarm and rebellion have broken out against either the arbitrary diminishment of these standards or their replacement by a merely aesthetic radicalism. For

me the history of religious life is at the center of the history of that inner-Christian rebellion; the tension between discipleship and the world, between the mystical and the political, remains rooted in the very heart of Christianity. The tension describes at once the greatness and the constitutional imperilment of Christianity; it characterizes its apocalyptic alarm. As I see it—and I need to elaborate on this—the alarm belongs to the spirit and mission of religious orders, even (and especially) today.

Let me illustrate the meaning of religious life, however sketchily, with a highly profane comparison.[8] In the world of film and television we are all familiar with the figure of the stuntman, the double who stands in when the story line turns dangerous, perhaps even life-threatening. Hardly anyone knows them, these profane "stand-ins." Invisibility and inconspicuousness belong to their profession, yet they are indispensable for risky productions. As I see it, Christianity is not some sort of postmodern sideshow, but rather the most perilous production of world history, since God Godself is involved in it. It is religious orders that step in whenever and wherever it turns particularly dangerous. *Historia docet.* What of the present? What does it mean when the Jesuit Jon Sobrino, who only by chance escaped the massacre of the Jesuits in El Salvador, immediately afterward came to Europe and just as matter-of-factly returned to an imperiled life with new community members?

In my view such standing-in during risky situations has something to do with the religious vows—for example, with the one that is especially controversial today, the vow of chastity. This vow easily becomes empty, stunting or psychologically distorted if it is not lived as a freedom, a freedom in the world and also in the church, a freedom that the world does not give. If nothing is wagered with the vows, but only something denied, they easily become masochistic. *Vita docet.*

Allow me in this context to repeat at the outset a concern about the vow of chastity already formulated in my first lecture to you in 1976: the vow should not have a eucharistic motivation, or more generally speaking an ecclesiological one; rather, it should have primarily an eschatological motivation. By this I repeat and single out a first, of course primarily inner-ecclesial, task for religious orders:

> If the evangelical counsel of celibacy has something to do with living hopefully in expectation of the second coming, must not the religious orders then claim this evangelical counsel more decisively for themselves? Surely they must press their claim to this charism—in its renewed and more radical form. Must they not see in the Church's institutionalization of celibacy for all priests a certain obfuscation of their specific and irreplaceable mission? Should not therefore the critical questioning of priestly celibacy perhaps be raised more by the religious orders than by so-called liberal critics inside and outside the Church? If the religious orders themselves were to raise the question in this way, might this not free the subject of mandatory celibacy, as pressing as it is emotionally overcharged, from all kinds of false alternatives and presuppositions?[9]

But now I will turn directly to the theme you have set for me. I do so tentatively, and conceding in advance the shortcomings in what I will say. What are the signs of the times and what is a prophetic-critical response for the religious orders? I would like to preface my response with at least two further remarks:

1. Christianity does not support any gnostic dualism between time and eternity, between creation and redemption. Of course, from the start it has had its problems with time and with the signs of the times. Again and again it has succumbed to the temptation to cover over the still-outstanding end of time and disappointed imminent expectation with the gnostic axiom of the atemporality of salvation and irredeemability of time, thinking about the God of Abraham, the God of Jesus, as if this God were a Platonic idea. This has been the case from Marcion right up to our own latter-day speculative gnosticisms and idealisms. Only since the most recent council has discourse about these signs of the times reentered the life of the church and of theology, requiring us to perceive them with the eyes of faith and to penetrate them with the

power of hope. They deserve my attention as well, though I will not speak in more detail here of those time-signs already widely discussed today—such as the frequently heard call for the preservation of creation, that is, the call for a praxis of ecological wisdom that has resounded ever since we discovered to our horror that, in our technological-economic progress, we have left one thing out of account: nature. A number of these rather well-known signs of the times will come up throughout this address (above all in part V, on mission perspectives). But first I will deal with a sign of the times that both engages and requires the very heart of religious life and, in the final analysis, of Christian identity itself.

2. Prophecy is not utopia; but it may also be true that prophecy is weaker and more indeterminate, gesturing helplessly in a time that is lacking in great visions, or does not even miss them; in a time of the absence of utopias, a time of broken-down, misused and disgraced utopias; in a time that resolutely avoids utopias—in short, in our own time. This issue will have to be taken up if, as you have asked, we are to describe a prophetic-critical response of religious orders to the signs of the times.

II. Religion, Yes—God, No

Some years ago a slogan circulated among us that reflected the mood of many, above all of many youths, many young Christians. It went like this: Jesus, yes—the church, no. If I were today to venture a diagnosis of this final decade of our century, an effort which admittedly would come from a theological perspective, yet be not only for the church but also for contemporary society, I would sum it up this way: Religion, yes—God, no. So the thing that would be required first and foremost of religious orders today (not as a doctrine but as a form of life) is something that is at the same time most elementary and most risky—witnessing to God in the midst of proreligious Godlessness, in an age of religion without God.

It is clear that the time of modernity's great and passionate atheists is over. But, as strange as it may sound, they still agreed with Christians on the seriousness of the God-question. Modernity's atheists contested the God-question above all in view of the world's abysmal history of suffering. They saw no possibility of sustaining the age-old theodicy question as an eschatological question.[10] However, it was precisely in this denial, in the passion of their critique of God, that they were still close to Christians.

In our world today the dispute no longer revolves around these atheistic issues. But does it have anything to do with God anymore? We are hearing and reading that it all has to do with religion. There is a new enthusiasm for religion, or more precisely a new enthusiasm for myths, that is popping up everywhere: first among intellectuals, but also among managers and the managed, among those who return from their electronically networked workplaces and whose imaginations need to recuperate from the faceless computer. Religion, as a compensatory myth of freedom, is on the rise in our still- or postmodern world. This religion's prophet is certainly not Jesus, but neither is it someone like Marx. Rather, if we are to cite one name as exemplary, it is Nietzsche. Last fall a German politician, obviously gripped by the dramatic upheavals in Eastern Europe, said "Marx is dead. Jesus lives." Well, that is more a confessional statement than a diagnostic one. As a diagnostic statement, at least for us in Western Europe (and probably much farther abroad), the most one might say is "Marx is dead; Nietzsche lives." And this does not make things any easier for Christians.

Religion is quite welcome today, as long as it presents itself only as something Dionysian, as the attainment of happiness through avoidance of suffering and mourning, as the soothing of our diffuse and rootless fears. Religion as a mythical enchantment of the soul, as a psychological-aesthetic claim of innocence for men and women, a religion that has silenced every eschatological disquietude with the dream of the return of the same or even, in still more religious fashion, with newly proliferating fantasies of transmigration or reincarnation of souls: religion in this sense is quite welcome. But what about God? What about the God of Abraham, Isaac and Jacob, who is also the God of Jesus?

III. The Beatitudes as Guides into the Passion for God

When I spoke to you in 1976, I essayed an interpretation of the three evangelical counsels.[11] This time I would like to say something about the Beatitudes from the Sermon on the Mount, in view of the witness to God required of religious life—selectively, of course, with a focus on our theme. As I see it, the Beatitudes are something like guides into the passion for God in the dual sense of the word passion: as ardor for God and as an avowed suffering unto God.

1. *"Blessed in God's eyes are the poor."*[12] I confess that meditation on this Beatitude permeates my theological biography. As early as 1962 a small book of mine appeared entitled *Poverty of Spirit.*[13] In it I focused on the difficulty, indeed the very possibility, of accepting oneself. When I published *Zeit der Orden?* in 1977, I stressed above all the inner connection between talk about biblical poverty and the actual poor themselves, who as we know were privileged by Jesus. Here I would like to sketch out a fundamental characteristic of this Beatitude that in my view relates directly to witnessing to God.[14] It is not by chance that this characteristic comes out of the Old Testament, Israelite background of Jesus' message. And that background cannot be dismissed or rejected as something superseded, even for the Christian witness to God.

No one knew this better than Paul (1 Cor 8:4). In the *Shema Israel*—"Hear, oh Israel, your God is one," from Dt 6:4—the name "God" is imposed upon human beings really for the first time and in a unique way. Here the confession of God breaks through into the religious history of humankind. As long as we are only dealing with "religion" (whatever that might mean in today's pro-religious world), we may certainly dispense with this tradition. But if we are dealing with *God* and also with *prayer,* then the experience of and passion for God articulated in this tradition is indispensable.[15]

I have often asked myself what it really is that distinguishes pre-Christian Israel, a small, culturally rather insignificant and politically voiceless desert people, from the glittering high cultures of its time, from Egypt, from Persia, from Greece? In my view it is a particular kind of defenselessness, of poverty; it is a certain way that Israel was incapable of successfully distancing itself from the contradictions, horrors and abysses of reality—by mythologizing or idealizing the conditions of its life, for example. Israel knew no mythical or ideational riches of spirit with which it could lift itself above its own fears, the alienation of exile, and the history of suffering that was continually breaking out in its midst. In its innermost essence, it remained mythically and ideally mute. Compared to the powerful and glamorously flourishing cultural landscapes of its time, Israel remained ultimately an eschatological "landscape of cries,"[16] a landscape of memory and expectation. It showed little aptitude for forgetting, and at the same time little capacity for automatic, idealistic processing of its disappointments. Even when it imported and mimicked a culturally foreign stock of myth and idealizing concepts, it was nonetheless never able to be definitively consoled by them. Thus one could almost say that Israel's election, its capacity for God, showed itself in a particular kind of incapacity: the incapacity to let itself be consoled by myths or ideas that are remote from history. This is precisely what I would call Israel's poverty before God, or poverty of spirit, that Jesus blessed.

Our Christian witness to God needs to be reminded of this in our mythically enthralled postmodern age. After all, this is also true for us: Whoever hears the message of the resurrection in such a way that the cry of the crucified has become inaudible in it, hears not the Gospel but rather a myth of the victor. Whoever hears the Christian message in such a way that in it there is nothing left to be expected, but only something that needs to be perceived and acknowledged, hears falsely. Not even Christology is without eschatological uneasiness, not even it is without that cry with which, as we all know, not only the Old Testament but also the New Testament ends: the cry we have since then mythically or idealistically silenced.

A trace of something unreconciled hovers over Christianity. To banish it would not be the expression of a strong faith, but rather of little faith. Do we believe in God, or do we believe in our faith in God, and in this perhaps really believe in ourselves, or in what we would like to think is true about us? But does not a faith that believes not only in itself, but in God, necessarily take the form of an incessant questioning in temporally charged expectation? Not vague or unfocused questions, but truly passionate and incessant questions belong to the passion for God with which we must come to terms today. Is there possibly too much singing and not enough crying out in our Christian spirituality? Too much rejoicing and too little mourning, too much acceptance and too little regret, too much comfort and too little hunger for consolation?

Thinking particularly of young people today, these questions seem to me to be the decisive ones for our witnessing to God. They are inspired by Jesus' first Beatitude, a Beatitude that is in no way meant only for an exhausted life, one looking only for some foothold and for security.[17]

2. *"Blessed are they who mourn"*…for they will be consoled, as the well-known conclusion goes. The will to power which has asserted itself in European modernity—over nature and also over other societies and cultures—has made mourning constitutionally foreign to us. Yet as the capacity to mourn wanes, so too does the capacity to allow oneself to be consoled, or to understand consolation as anything more than empty promises. After all, as the philosopher Theodor Adorno so rightly interpreted a passage from Kierkegaard, "The step from mourning into consolation is not the biggest, but the smallest."[18]

Mourning is in no way foreign to the Christian witness to God. How could it be? After all, to mourn obviously means to sense something as substantively absent. Does this mean: to sense God's absence? Absolutely! That sense of absence plays between mourning and hope. Only because of a sort of Christian delusion of perfection and reconciliation have we convinced ourselves that mourning ought to be something foreign to us. For me such a delusion is finally nothing less than a symptom of the senescence of a Christianity that tries to compensate for its unadmitted fears by overaffirmation, by whistling in the dark. Mourning, however, is not at all an attack of weak hope, unless one misunderstands hope as some sort of Pollyannaish optimism. Mourning is hope in resistance—resisting the frenetic acceleration of time in which we are more and more losing ourselves; resisting forgetting and the forgetfulness of the forgotten that goes by the names of progress and development among us; resisting the attempt to reduce to existential insignificance everything that has vanished into the past and cannot be brought back. Finally, in other words, hope resists the attempt to expel a sense for what is absent from our wisdom about ourselves.

But is such a sense of absence at all consoling? And does not the biblical God will above all to be this: comfort for those who have collapsed in suffering, relief for those who are driven by existential anxiety? Here, in my view, everything depends on not misunderstanding the biblical promises of consolation. Our secularized modernity has been able neither to respond to the longing for consolation, nor to do away with it. Accordingly, today we are offered—in a quasipostmodern way—myths and fairy tales purported to have the potential to console. And it is clear that a perplexed Christianity has a deeply rooted susceptibility to these myths and fairy tales. Have we left ourselves, and others, in the dark about the biblical meaning of consolation?

The God of Jesus does not make one unhappy. But does that God make one happy? Does God respond to our expectations of happiness? These should in no way be misanthropically denounced. What we have to be clear about is that today, however, certain expectations of happiness are becoming increasingly widespread and influential that do not recognize any "happiness that includes pain,"[19] nor any happiness having an undercurrent of suffering or mourning. Rather they promote the individual's happiness, using strategies that avoid suffering and mourning.

Does God make one happy in this sense? in the sense of a happiness free of longing and suffering? Was Israel ever happy in this sense with Yahweh? Was Jesus ever happy in this sense with his Father? Does a biblically grounded religion make one happy in this sense? Does it offer one serene self-reconciliation, an indwelling with ourselves without any fears or rebellion, a knowledge of self in which there is no sense of absence? Does it answer questions? Does it fulfill one's wishes, at least the most ardent ones? I am not so sure.

But then why God? Why then our prayer? To ask God for God is, in the end, what Jesus has to say to his disciples concerning prayer. At any rate, this is how I read the central teaching about prayer in Lk 11:1–13, especially v. 13. Strictly speaking, he promises no other consolation. At any rate, his promise of comfort does not displace us into a mythical realm of serene harmony and unproblematic, identity-reinforcing peace with oneself.

In his book on the priesthood, Eugen Drewermann offers the opinion that in our culture there is probably only one group of persons we could associate with Jesus' noncomformist lifestyle. He names the poets, and points to Goethe's elegies, Rilke's sonnets and Stefan Zweig's novels. But here we part company.

As I was preparing this text I was reminded of another figure, the figure of my teacher, Karl Rahner. Above and beyond being my teacher and friend, to me he had become my father in faith. In a sermon I preached on the fiftieth anniversary of his ordination, this is how I tried to speak of him, a religious, and to explain his type of existential nonconformism:

> A father in faith—and himself homeless. Thus were they—indeed, thus are all—these fathers in faith, these servants of God, in the Abrahamic traditions, in the Pauline traditions, in the Ignatian traditions. In them appear the traces of that messianic homelessness of the Son that has been handed down to us from the Gospel....Karl Rahner never interpreted Christianity for us as a kind of bourgeois domestic religion from which every hope threatened by death, every vulnerable and stubborn longing has been expelled. I never felt his understanding of faith to be a kind of ideology of security, or solemn elevation of the state of affairs attained to this point, however progressive it be. Always there remains a homelessness, through everything there remains a

longing, which I never felt to be sentimental, never Pollyannaish
or naively optimistic, but rather more a kind of silent sigh of the
creature, like a wordless cry for light before the hidden face of
God. If I am right, this longing has not become easier to bear in his
old age. Rather, even more inexpressible, even more melancholy,
more burdensome. Yes, oppressive longing, defenseless homelessness! Because the journey is not at an end, and the weariness is
great; because too many ashes already cover the dim embers of
life, and no storm from paradise kindles them anew; because a
growing sense of futility can lay open the heaviness of this longing
for God...[20]

In this way Karl Rahner has become for me—and for many,
especially many young people—a witness to God in these times.
An essential part of handing on the faith today is bringing the history of life and the history of faith together as he did. Here is
where the life of the larger church always threatens to founder,
and this is also what—let this not be denied here—those theologies oriented by depth psychology are striving for.

3. *"Blessed are they who hunger and thirst after justice..."* Blessed
are they who hunger and thirst for that universal justice of God
that applies to everyone, to the living and the dead, to suffering
present and past. Passionate interest in this undivided justice of
God is a constitutive part of witnessing to God. It is at the same
time mystical and political: mystical, because it does not give up
its interest in the salvation of past, unreconciled suffering; political, because it is precisely this interest in universal justice that
continually commits it to justice among the living. It is not the
case that, only after the eschatological God in postmodern fashion is made to disappear, religion is made capable of being political; rather does religion then become totally and completely
apolitical, robbed completely of its prophetic and social-critical
power.

Christian witnessing to God is guided through and through by
political spirituality, a political mysticism. Not a mysticism of political power and political domination, but rather—to speak

metaphorically—a mysticism of open or opened eyes. Not only the ears for hearing, but also the eyes are organs of grace! Jesus is not Buddha! With all respect for Eastern mysticism and spirituality, let me stress that. In the end Jesus did not teach an ascending mysticism of closed eyes, but rather a God-mysticism with an increased readiness for perceiving, a mysticism of open eyes, which sees more and not less. It is a mysticism that especially makes visible all invisible and inconvenient suffering, and—convenient or not— pays attention to it and takes responsibility for it, for the sake of a God who is a friend to human beings.

When it comes to God and salvation, of course, we are only too glad to put our money on what is invisible and imperceptible, on invisible grace. But clearly Jesus insisted on visibility and on the obligation to perceive—for example, in the parable of the Good Samaritan, or in the criteria of the last judgment in the "little apocalypse" (from Mt 25)—and this to our continual amazement: "Lord, when did we see you naked, hungry or in prison…?"

Such witnessing to God is not allowed political innocence. In the end, witness is intimately involved, with eyes that see, in that history where people are crucified and tortured, hated and miserly loved; and no mythos far-removed from history, no world-blind gnosis, can give it back the innocence that is lost in such an historical trial. The God who comes near in Jesus obviously is not primarily interested in how and what we think about him, but rather first in how we behave toward the other; and only in this— how we deal with others—can it be known how we think about God and what we think of God.

IV. Becoming a Self in the Presence of Others

The witness to God we are discussing here, the passion for God that I hold to be the elementary critical-prophetic task of religious orders today, obviously requires strong subjects in which the history of life and history of faith are authentically integrated, not pitted against one another in a superego-like fashion (a sure recipe for neurosis). Here the advice and assistance of psychology can be quite useful for successfully integrating one's life with one's faith. Its critical and therapeutic objections absolutely deserve to be heard, as long as psychology for its part does not present itself as a substitute religion and theology, and as long as it is aware of its own one-sidedness and blindspots. But is it aware of these?

For the political theologian in me, a thoroughly depth-psychological theology has an effect on religious life that is too apolitical; more precisely it is too enamored with the self. In the end it proves itself to be the very narcissism for which it is supposed to provide therapy. It suggests that there are religious depths in the self, abysses to which dreams provide the key; whereas in truth superficiality and shallowness prevail, as long as the self does not experience and prove itself in the presence of others, with others, for others. Perhaps becoming a self in the presence of others is not so important when it comes to modest hopes; but it is indispensable for the grand hopes, the ones that shape our lives. They demand a self set on fire in the presence of and with others. At least that is what is taught by the primordial biblical history of how subjects come into being.[21] The primordial design of the church is rooted not on the basis of observances, or of subordination, or notions of office; but rather because of the hope that is given to us and which no one can hope for him- or herself alone. This is the basic outline for the *vita communis,* without which the eschatological hope of Christians does not exist. It is not the isolated time of one's own life that forms the matrix for this hope, but much more the time of others; it is not only one's own end in death, but rather others', the deaths of others, that keeps eschatological suspense awake in one's own heart.

Everything having to do with Jesus is geared toward that. His images and visions of the reign of God—of a comprehensive peace among men and women and nature in the presence of God, of a home and a father, of a kingdom of peace, of justice and of reconciliation, of tears wiped away and of the laughter of the children of God—cannot be hoped for only with oneself in view and for oneself alone. None of them inspire confidence only for oneself, in some kind of isolated transcendence inward, so to speak. In believing that others can rely on them, in communicating them to others and hoping them "for others," they belong to oneself as well. Only then. That is true for the radicality of eschatological hope, but also for conversion, which in its depths only succeeds where it is deemed possible for others and offered to others. Here is not simply an apology for an institution that ignores the self or reinforces the superego, nor a disguised rhetoric for obedience. On the contrary, hope for others and thus for myself provides authentic criteria for a critique of all institutional phenomena leading to the isolation of self, the flight from self, and consequently into a problematic openness of the self to being dominated by others. The strong self, the strong subject of hope and witness to God, is a *plurale tantum*.[22]

In the sixties and early seventies, a time pregnant with utopias, we always had to be careful that our eschatological hope was not simply replaced with no further ado by a utopia to which, as everyone knew, nobody prays or cries out. Now we are facing a new problem, one in my view even more pressing, especially from the perspective of religious life. In our still- or postmodern age, in which utopias have shriveled up or are rejected, and visions are renounced or waste away, vocations committed absolutely to include a way of life that has not yet been lived can hardly be explained or justified anymore, or only with greatest difficulty. No wonder it is precisely today that, even within the church and theology, a suspicion has surfaced that the life of the vows has some delusional characteristics, or at least always runs the risk of them.

Only religious communities that do not simply reject this suspicion out-of-hand may raise a counterquestion or voice something like a countersuspicion. By what criteria for normalcy and for spiritual health and maturity is religious life being evaluated? Why not see religious life as one form of life—certainly not the only one, but an exemplary one—that stands against the unconfessed delusions of our "enlightened" life-world?

Is there not today something like a growing delusion of innocence or unaccountability, a voyeuristic mentality, something like
Pilate's delusion? It is not a will to power, certainly, though only
because it really does not will anything at all, outside itself and its
own innocence. And does not such a delusion strike at the very
substance not only of opting for faith, but of opting for humanity
in general? I can try to clarify what I mean in this way: the market
mentality, the exchange mentality that is becoming universal eco-
nomically today, is no longer limited only to the economy. Now it
encroaches not only upon the autonomy of political life, but also
reaches the foundations of our spiritual life. That is to say, everything now appears to be exchangeable, and interchangeable,
even interpersonal relationships and our life commitments. You
have only lived if you have lived several times. If there are life-
options at all anymore, they exist only as options with provision-
ary clauses. There is commitment, if at all, only as commitment
with the right to return and refund:[23] "Here I stand, I can also do
otherwise. I never follow only my own opinion. Anything goes,
even the opposite…" "Anything at all" goes its quiet way. Can
humanity go its own way like that?

In my view, questions and perspectives such as these can and
should be made clear to young people today. As I see it, it is not
the strong, mature subjects who have adapted themselves to such
a mentality of exchange, but the weak and immature, who ultimately only contribute to the increasing power of the illusion of
acceleration we today euphorically call development. If the idea
of the vows is to be saved for young people, if the binding character of the vows is not to be surrendered to the suspicion that they
are really only livable for a life that has become exhausted and in
a sense old before its time, then such questions and perspectives,
thoroughly social-critical and liberating ones, must be raised.
Against their backdrop it might become clear that religious life
need not drown in a worldless, humorless and sectarian fundamentalism, wherein one instinctively lives only with the like-
minded and defends oneself against unconscious fears and
anxieties by means of a zealously honed way of speaking and

thinking. The fears that haunt our still- or post-modern souls are probably rooted entirely elsewhere—for example, in the sense of being abandoned to the intergalactic cold of an infinitely indifferent evolution completely outside our control, in which something or other voicelessly runs its course....[24]

V. Mission Perspectives

I will try to diagnose the fundamental situation of the church today, in order to arrive at some perspectives and loci for a mission for contemporary religious. Today the church stands in a highly complex situation that almost pulls in two different directions at once: for the first time it is on the way to become a truly global church; at the same time, all over the globe, and not least in Europe, it finds itself more and more in minority status, in a global diaspora that in almost an unprecedented way forces it back to the heart of its mission. I might add that this characterization of the situation holds as well (at this general level) for the present state of all Christianity.

1. *Conviviality, Cultural and Social.* From the perspective of today's church becoming global, two central tasks present themselves that in my view cannot be accomplished without the living contribution of the religious orders. What is more, these two tasks extend deeply into social and cultural life.

The first concerns the formation of a cultural polycentrism within the church, without which there cannot be a truly global church, and without which the aims of the Second Vatican Council would have to remain unrealized.[25] Inculturation has arrived, in a previously unimagined and scarcely ever practiced way, discovering the world with the eyes of Jesus. Elsewhere I have spoken in more detail about the theological problematic of the processes of inculturation, the misunderstandings that accompany them, and especially the challenges that they entail for European Christianity.[26] Here let me recall only the questions about the subjects and loci of this inculturation.

The primary subjects and loci, as I see it, are the particular regional and local churches themselves. Precisely because many of our religious orders are not organized on a national but on an international basis, not on a regional but on a global basis, would they and their cloisters not be the natural seedbed for productive intercultural exchange, rather than serving only as training centers for the old European mentality? Could they not be the first dwelling places for a conviviality between different cultural worlds? Would it not be necessary in our monastic forms of life, even their liturgical and pastoral publicness, to see, experience and learn productive exchange—indeed, to see them also as the prototype for a European community that will never be purely European again? As I said earlier, the vows must not only avoid something, but must risk something: for example, the experiment of this kind of conviviality.

Today, probably more than ever before, a global church consciousness must deal with the fact that the church lives in the intersection between the rich and poor nations of earth. As the church becomes global, a particularly challenging task arises for religious orders; it can be seen in the change in mentality that is spreading here and throughout Europe (as well as in North America): a growing everyday postmodernism in our hearts that threatens once again to remove the so-called third world into a faceless distance. In 1992, who among us does not think primarily of the European Common Market and the new opportunities opening up in Central and Eastern Europe? And if we in Europe think about Columbus at all during the quincentennial (1492–1992), do we not do so exclusively from our own perspective and in the light of our European interests? Is there not currently something like an intellectual *[geistige]* strategy for immunizing Europe, a tendency toward mental isolationism, a cult of new innocence in an attempt to withdraw ourselves from global challenges, a new variant of what I once called "tactical provincialism"?

What we could characterize philosophically as postmodern thought—the rejection of universal categories and of universal morality, thinking in terms of difference and dissent, with scaled-down standards and in glittering fragments—has a quite problematic, everyday parallel. Is there not a new mood that places the need and misery of poor nations at a greater existential distance from us? Is there not a new kind of privatization spreading among us, a spectator-mentality with no obligation to perceive critically, a rather voyeuristic way of dealing with the great scenes of crisis and suffering in the world? Are there not in our enlightened Europe more and more symptoms of a second immaturity *[Unmündigkeit]* in our dealings with the great crises in our world? Such immaturity is clearly fed by the impression that today we are more informed than ever about everything, particularly about the things that threaten us and about all the crises and horrors in the world; but the step from knowing to acting, from information to praxis, has never seemed so great and never so unlikely as it does today. Is not a mentality growing among us that has gotten used to crisis and misery? We have become accustomed to crises of poverty in the world that seem to be becoming ever more commonplace and that we therefore delegate, with helpless shrug, to a subjectless social evolution. When Francis Fukuyama, the acting director of the American State Department's planning staff, presented his sensational thesis last year on the "end of history" (according to which the United States, having won the cold war, has become the final stage of modern history in general), he had more or less forgotten the third world.[27]

For the church, however, the painful reality of these poor nations, one that cries out to heaven, has gradually become a question of its own future and a touchstone for its existence as a global church. In the final analysis it is not just that the church *has* a third-world church; it now largely *is* such a church, with an inalienable European history of origin. Faced with large-scale misery that cries out to heaven—or no longer cries out, because it long ago lost its capacity to speak or to dream—the church cannot comfort itself by thinking we have here simply a tragedy wherein, in a world growing ever more rapidly together, some countries are behind the times. Nor by thinking that these poor are merely the victims or hostages of their own pitiless oligarchies. What was said in the language of earliest Christianity, made up of wandering prophets and Christians in small villages, must be spelled out and taken seriously by a global church: "What you did to the least of these.…"

Therefore, the European church must not allow itself, in a quasi-postmodern way, to be talked out of its standards or allow them to be whittled down under the pressure of circumstances. It may not remove itself from the tension between the mystical and the political into an ahistorical, mythological mentality. To be sure, the church is not primarily a moral institution, but rather the bearer of hope, and its theology is not primarily an ethics, but rather an eschatology. Yet precisely therein lies the root of its power, even in powerlessness, not to surrender its standards of responsibility and solidarity, not to consign the preferential option for the poor simply to the poor churches alone. All this has to do with the greatness and the burden laid upon us by the biblical word *God*. It does not distance us from the social and political life of others; it only removes the basis for hatred and violence. And it calls all men and women to walk uprightly, precisely in order that all might freely bend the knee and give thanks with joyful hearts.

The witness to God of the religious orders, of which we have already spoken so much, means also trying to break through the new mentality of isolation and diminishing standards in a prophetic-critical way. To put it bluntly, religious orders must more than ever practice not just a modest responsibility, a modest solidarity among ourselves, but rather also not lose sight of the monumental responsibility, the capacious solidarity (reaching across the global abyss separating poor from rich) that many today would like to dismiss as abstract. But how else shall the church overcome the unvoiced doubts of its poor? Supported by a heartfelt readiness for poverty, religious orders need to keep the encompassing solidarity alive and available, and build it up strong, to counter the mentality of isolation I have described. In the poor nations themselves, the primary task of the religious orders' witness to God will be their social conviviality in being with the poor in the base communities.

2. *The Pastoral Situation of the Diaspora.* The church and Christianity in global diaspora, especially in Europe: here too there is a challenge for religious orders. The emergence of a new idea of Europe can without hesitation be counted as one of the contemporary signs of the times. But how should we deal with it?

More and more attention is being devoted to the issue, even in ecclesial circles. John Paul II has already announced a special meeting of the episcopal synods of Europe. Talk about a "new evangelization" of Europe is making the rounds. Can this be guided by a vision of a quasipremodern, pre-Reformation European West? I very much doubt it. It is certainly true that Christianity is structurally integrated into the history and spirit of Europe. But how can we avoid the impression that, while Christianity belongs certainly with the presuppositions to and historical and cultural background-assumptions of the European spirit, it does not in any substantive way belong to Europe's contemporary life? How do we free Christianity in Europe from the clutches of its utter historicization?[28]

I would like to respond to this problem first in view of our new pastoral-diaspora situation, and then in view of a witness to God for the sake of the salvation of the human person.

It is obvious that we must reckon with a growing diaspora situation for Christianity and the church in Europe. We start from the fact that the widespread popular church[29] structures in Europe are disappearing at an accelerating rate (even if this process in its particulars may be more hidden here in Germany than elsewhere). A more and more pressing requirement for the survival of living Christianity in Europe is new forms of life, new patterns of a Christian *vita communis,* in which eschatological hope will continue to find a dwelling place.

In my earlier reflections on religious life, I warned that religious orders must not allow themselves simply to be fit into the preformulated pastoral plans for a greater church—plans into which they could have had no input—no matter how reasonable they sound.[30] Today I would like to urge the religious orders to immerse themselves more and more into the pastoral situation of the diaspora in Europe. For example, in France it is the monastic communities that are creating new structures of life in the spiritual wastelands of our giant cities and in the posturban monstrosities of our industrial world, new structures whereby they can be closer to persons who are no longer visible to typically parish-oriented thinking or the paternalistic structures of the popular church.[31] A new evangelization of Europe can only happen in this way. And for this task the orders can and must allow themselves to be mobilized on a broader front, if (as I said earlier) their vows indeed mean not only that something is to be avoided or copied, but that something is to be ventured.

3. *Witness to God Against the Death of the Person.* Deep is the trail that religious life—since Benedict of Nursia—has carved into the history of the European spirit. Has it now come to an end? Has it faded away once and for all? Is it now nothing but the signature of a glorious past, given over only to historical or aesthetic appreciation? Rather, the existence of religious orders is indispensable even today as a passionate and in no way merely private articulation of the possibility of God in this age.

Let me recall Nietzsche yet again. As we all know, he suggested that we place the course of time consistently against the horizon of the death of God; only in this way would we finally be able to understand what awaits us. Yet, as he says in *Ecce Homo,* "I know my fate. One day my name will be associated with the memory of something tremendous—a crisis without equal on earth, the most profound collision of conscience, a decision that was conjured up against everything that had been believed, demanded, hallowed so far."[32]

Nietzsche did not think of himself as one of the typical representatives of modern atheism, whose thinking is continually captivated by the very thing against which it is striving. He understood himself as someone who consistently carried through the message of the death of God; and the unavoidable consequence of the death of God for him was this: man, as we have learned to recognize him historically up until now, with his values and his ideals, this man, too, has been left behind. Accordingly, Nietzsche spoke again and again of the abolition of man. He spoke of the death of the subject; he held the subject to be a mere fiction, and talk about the *I* to be an anthropomorphism. He prophesied and demanded an end to normative-moral consciousness, in a life beyond good and evil wherein the successor to the human being, the overman, would be nothing other than his own unending experiment. And he proclaimed the end of historical consciousness, since time, unshackled from the idea of God, plunges into an anonymous evolution that intends nothing but evolution, nothing but that infinite finitude against which Nietzsche mustered his "most profound idea," the idea of the eternal return of the same. Thus Nietzsche not only anticipated many of today's postmodern certitudes, he also unveiled the naiveté of the modern critique of religion, which thought it could only set the power and greatness of the modern subject free by abandoning the idea of God. He shrewdly made the connection between the death of God and the death of the human person that European modernity still managed to presuppose was intact and endowed with its ideals of freedom and maturity.

And so, looking back over the course of time, the decisive alternative becomes clear: either the polytheistic-aesthetic gods of postmodernity, or the biblical God; either Dionysus, or the God of Abraham, Isaac and Jacob, who is also the God of Jesus.

We can go with Nietzsche, turning our backs on the man of Europe's past, into the mythical-Dionysian realm of the exalted one he called the overman—beyond good and evil, divorced from memory, suffering, and mourning—above all innocent, being cheerfully and serenely embedded in the eternal return of the same. His most trivial realization is probably the most suggestive: man as computerized intelligence, as an intelligence without history, without any capacity to suffer and without morality; in short, a rhapsody of innocence concretized into a smoothly functioning machine.

Or we can place the threshold of the future against the counterhorizon—admittedly ever more weakly illuminated—of the idea of God; that is, risk the decision to turn back from Nietzsche, who had so shrewdly made the connection between the death of God and the dwindling-away of the human person historically entrusted to our care. Of course, our resolve can only succeed and be argumentatively sustained if it can fall back upon a form of life. Therefore, resistance to the death of man[33] must be rooted in the passion for God that has been the central focus of these reflections. I do not know of a more fundamental response to the signs of the times.

VI. *The End of Time*

Among the most telling signs of the times for me is not only the fact that we are asking and thinking about signs, but that we are asking and thinking about time itself. For some years now, dozens of books have been taking up the theme. Could it possibly be the ungrasped essence of time itself that makes us uneasy on all sides, that has become the secret source of the awkwardness and unadmitted fears of our oh-so-enlightened and progressive lives? All current opinions on the subject notwithstanding, it is precisely the biblically-motivated apocalypticists who trust time—quite simply because they know hopefully, and hope knowingly, that time has an end and that this end has a name, so time does not collapse into an empty, monotonous, infinite finitude, and we into it.[34]

Religious life would be livable, and worth living, in the spirit of such a serene and composed apocalypticism—for the sake both of God and of human beings. Even today.

Notes

IN PLACE OF A FOREWORD/
INTRODUCTION: READING METZ

1. [The *Paulus-Gesellschaft* is an organization of theologians and scientists founded in 1955 to facilitate interaction between their two fields. In the 1960s it also brought together theologians and Marxist intellectuals to discuss their commonalities and differences under the rubric of humanism. The members of the Frankfurt School to whom Metz refers are Theodor Adorno, Max Horkheimer, Herbert Marcuse and also, more distantly, Walter Benjamin. (Though he had died during the Second World War, Benjamin's works were collected and published through the efforts of his friends Adorno and Horkheimer.)— *Trans.*]

2. *The Mystical Element of Religion,* 2 volumes (New York: E. P. Dutton, 1909), I:50–82.

3. *Ibid.,* I:53.

4. This notion of a force-field or constellation comes ultimately from one of Metz's favorite thinkers, Theodor Adorno. I learned it from Martin Jay, who himself uses it in his introduction to Adorno's thought. See, Martin Jay, *Adorno* (Cambridge, MA: Harvard University Press, 1984), 14f.

5. "Productive Noncontemporaneity," in *Observations on "The Spiritual Situation of the Age,"* ed. Jürgen Habermas, trans. with an introduction by Andrew Buchwalter (Cambridge, MA: MIT Press, 1984), 171.

6. *Ibid.*

7. As indicated in the title of the Habermas *Festschrift: Philosophical Interventions in the Unfinished Project of Enlightenment,* ed. Axel Honneth, Thomas McCarthy et al., trans. William Rehg (Cambridge, MA: MIT Press, 1992). To be sure, Metz does not fully accept Habermas' proposal; he remains far more sympathetic to Habermas' predecessors in the Frankfurt School, Theodor Adorno and Max Horkheimer.

8. See chapter 7, below.

9. See below, 32.

10. His first book, *Christliche Anthropozentrik,* argued even more. There he argued that the turn to the subject did not emerge in modernity *against* the Spirit of Christianity. Metz attempted to show that the beginnings of the turn to the subject can be found in the thought of Thomas Aquinas, who, for his part, was only completing the transformation of the cosmocentric categories of Graeco-Hellenic thought that was required if it was to be used to articulate and reflect on Christian revelation.

11. See below (chap. 2), and "Kirchliche Autorität im Anspruch der Freiheitsgeschichte," in Metz, Moltmann and Oellmüller, *Kirche im Prozeß der Aufklärung* (München: Kaiser-Grünewald, 1970), 63; also, *Faith in History and Society: Toward a Practical Fundamental Theology,* translated by David Smith (New York: Crossroad, 1980), 53f.

12. *Faith in History and Society,* 60.

13. A more extended and detailed argument that Metz's later work is still a fundamental theology in the form of a theological anthropology, and that the three categories of memory, solidarity and narrative are an alternative set of *existentialia,* is presented in my book, *Interruptions: Mysticism, Politics and Theology in the Work of Johann Baptist Metz* (forthcoming, Notre Dame Press).

14. See *Faith in History and Society,* chap. 10.

15. The early attempt to move within the domain of Rahner's theology is most evident in the changes that Metz made when preparing Rahner's foundational works, *Spirit in the World* and *Hearers of the Word,* for republication in the early sixties. The

changes he made reflected concerns he made explicit later. First, he worried that Rahner's ontology was not sensitive enough to the sociality of human existence (which he distinguishes from the *interpersonality* of human existence articulated by the concept of the I-Thou). Second, he gradually came to share the same conviction about Rahner's notion of historicity that he did of its usage in Heidegger's thought: "*a curious unhistoricity and artificiality* adheres to Heidegger's concept of history" (from "Heidegger und das Problem des Metaphysik," *Scholastik* 28 (1953), 12, n. 11, emphasis in original).

16. See "Do We Miss Karl Rahner?", below, page 103. Metz has given Rahner such praise since at least 1974; see "Karl Rahner— ein theologisches Leben. Theologie als mystische Biographie eines Christen-menschen heute," in *Stimmen der Zeit*, May 1974, translated in *Faith in History and Society*, 219–28.

17. *Ibid.*, 104.

18. See Ignacio Ellacuría, "The Crucified People," in *Mysterium Liberationis: Fundamental Concepts of Liberation Theology*, edited by Ignacio Ellacuría and Jon Sobrino (Maryknoll, N.Y.: Orbis, 1993), 580–603. As will become clear, I have found very close and mutually illuminating parallels between Metz, Sobrino and Ellacuría, all of whom knew and admired the work of Rahner, all of whom have struggled in the course of their careers to articulate something new, on the other side of the epistemological break brought about by the experience of crucified peoples. For a trenchant instance of this in Sobrino's work, see "Theology in a Suffering World: Theology as *Intellectus Amoris*," in *The Principle of Mercy: Taking the Crucified People from the Cross* (Maryknoll, N.Y.: 1994), 27–46.

19. This translates *Leiden an Gott*. Some comment is called for on this translation of what is undoubtedly *the* pivotal term in Metz's theological vocabulary. Usually in German the construction, *Leiden an...*can be translated simply "to suffer from...," as in, "to suffer from a cold." I have chosen a more unusual rendering in order to avoid the passive connotation of suffering "from" something. It is helpful in this regard to keep in mind that *Leiden*

an Gott is closely corollated with *Rückfragen an Gott,* which I have usually translated as "turning one's questioning back to God," or "insistent questioning of God." Thus, "suffering unto God" is both a passive *and* an active spiritual disposition. To "suffer unto God" denotes a spiritual disposition in which suffering, either that suffering that I experience, or others' suffering that I perceive in the present, or *remember and keep in mind* from the past, drives me toward God, crying out, protesting, questioning. Its Old Testament exemplar is Job, and the New Testament exemplar is Jesus, particularly as presented in the Gospel of Mark.

20. Both Benjamin and Bloch had long championed apocalyptic resources from the Jewish and Christian traditions in their idiosyncratic revisions of Marxist thought. Bloch's second major book dealt with Thomas Müntzer, and the rebellious Job of the Hebrew Bible was a recurring hero in his later works. Benjamin is well known for his desire to bring together Jewish Kabbalah (which he studied with Gershom Scholem) and Marxist materialism.

21. This was set as early as the late thirties, when he wrote his essay, "The Ignatian Mysticism of Joy in the World," in *Theological Investigations III: The Theology of the Spiritual Life* (New York: Crossroad, 1982), 277–93. The original text dates from 1937. It is instructive to note here that the primary figures Rahner draws on for interpreting Ignatius are from the tradition of Christian Neoplatonism: Bonaventure, Clement of Alexandria, Origen.

22. Ignacio Ellacuría, "Las Iglesias latinoamericanas interpelan a la Iglesia de España," *Sal Terrae* 826 (1982), 230. Cited in Jon Sobrino, *Jesus the Liberator: A Historical-Theological Reading of Jesus of Nazareth,* trans. by Paul Burns and Francis McDonagh (Maryknoll, N.Y.: Orbis, 1993), 262f. It is quite appropriate to use liberation theologians to interpret and complement Metz's theology, since he himself has pointed to their work as the fulfillment of his own theological agenda.

23. See "The Church and the World in the Light of a 'Political Theology,'" in *Theology of the World,* trans. William Glen-Doepel (New York: Herder & Herder, 1969), 107–24; also "Prophetic Authority," in Metz, Moltmann and Oelmüller, *Religion and Politi-*

cal Society, translated and edited by the Institute of Christian Thought (New York: Harper Forum Books, 1974).

24. See *Followers of Christ: The Religious Life and the Church,* trans. Thomas Linton (London/New York: Burns & Oates/ Paulist Press, 1978).

25. *Poverty of Spirit,* trans. John Drury (New York: Paulist, 1968).

1. THE NEW POLITICAL THEOLOGY

1. *Glaube in Geschichte und Gesellschaft* [Mainz: Matthias-Grünewald; the first, 1977 German edition was translated by David Smith and published as *Faith in History and Society: Toward a Practical Fundamental Theology* (New York: Seabury, 1980). This chapter translates the foreword to the fifth edition.—*Trans.*]

2. See J. B. Metz, *Zur Theologie der Welt* (Mainz, 1968; trans. *Theology of the World*), in which the ideas leading to a new political theology were gathered for the first time; also the volume edited by Helmut Peukert, *Diskussion zur 'politischen Theologie'* (Mainz, 1969).

3. I would like to express my thanks to those authors whose works are collected in the volume edited by Eduard Schillebeeckx, *Mystik und Politik. Theologie im Ringen um Geschichte und Gesellschaft* (Mainz, 1988). Many points of contact appeared in their works, as well as further encouragement to continue our common theological task.

4. I have spoken of three competing theological paradigms in my essay, "On the Way to a Postidealist theology" (see below, chap. 2): a neoscholastic, a transcendental-idealist, and a postidealist approach. In this context the new political theology, as well as the theological core of liberation theology, belongs to the postidealist approach. See also my foreword to the new (German) edition of Gustavo Gutiérrez's *A Theology of Liberation* (Mainz, 1992).

5. The Marxist challenge to theology is explicitly discussed as well in "On the Way to a Postidealist Theology" (see below, chap. 2). For the confrontation between political theology and

fundamental Marxist positions, see also "Nochmals: die marxistis-
che Herausforderung," in *Gottes Zukunft—Zukunft der Welt*
(München, 1986), 414–22, and "Politische Theologie und die
Herausforderung des Marxismus," in P. Rottländer (ed.), *Theologie der Befreiung und Marxismus*, 2. Aufl. (Münster, 1987), 175–86.

6. The discussions in my book, *The Emergent Church: The
Future of Christianity in a Postbourgeois World*, trans. Peter Mann
(New York: Crossroad, 1987), in *Unterbrechungen* (Gütersloh,
1982), and in the volume I published in collaboration with F.-X.
Kaufmann, *Zukunftsfähigkeit: Suchbewegungen im Christentum*
(Freiburg, 1987), are all shaped by the formulation of the issues
sketched out here, although with different accents. Further differentiations of the question of the subject within the ecclesial
realm may be found in my contribution "Das Konzil—'der
Anfang eines Anfangs'?", in K. Richter (ed.), *Das Konzil war erst
der Anfang* (Mainz, 1991), and in my introduction to the new edition of Karl Rahner's *Strukturwandel der Kirche als Aufgabe und
Chance* (Freiburg, 1989).

7. See chapter 10, below, on "becoming a self in the presence of
and with the other" as the anthropological premise of postidealist
theology. The essay also treats of the coprimordiality of perceiving
self and other, of self-acknowledgment and acknowledgment of the
other—that is, it treats of an identity for oneself that is always
indebted to an understanding of the other. Such fundamental
anthropological premises differentiate this theology from transcendental theology. Indeed, there is no theory of intersubjectivity or
alterity in Karl Rahner's foundational anthropological reflections.
The idea of absolute love of neighbor first surfaces in his Christology, and even there not at the beginning of his incarnational theology, developed as it is with such incomparable speculative power. To
be sure, Rahner speaks of that "other in which the immutable God
can be mutable"; yet, following the sense of his argument, that other
(which brings Hegel to mind, and not just terminologically) may
not be thought of as a person's being-an-other, not as a subject's
alterity to God!

8. See "Anamnestic Reason: A Theologian's Remarks on the

Crisis in the *Geisteswissenschaften*" in Honneth, McCarthy, et al. eds., *Cultural-Political Interventions in the Unfinished Project of Enlightenment* (Cambridge, MA: MIT Press, 1992), 189–94; "Freedom in Solidarity," in J. B. Metz & Jürgen Moltmann, *Faith and the Future: Essays on Theology, Solidarity, and Modernity*, with an introduction by Francis Schüssler Fiorenza (Maryknoll, N.Y.: Orbis, 1995), 72–78.

9. Here the following texts are particularly important: "Wohin ist Gott, wohin denn der Mensch?" in *Zukunftsfähigkeit*; "Wider die Zweite Unmündigkeit," in Rüsen, Lämmert & Glotz (eds.), *Zukunft der Aufklärung* (Frankfurt, 1988), 81–87. See also chapters 4 and 10 below.

10. [*Eingedenken*. In German, the adverb *eingedenk* means "in remembrance of," and it is used in that sense in the Order of Mass: "Do this in remembrance of me." I have attempted to follow Metz's usage by constructing the verbal form "remembrancing."—*Trans.*]

11. On the early onset of this "halving of the spirit of Christianity," and on the problem of the "Hellenization of Christianity" associated with it, besides the reflections in "Anamnestic Reason" (n. 8), see also "Löscht den jüdischen Geist nicht aus," in Krüggeler, Junker, Möhler (eds.), *Löscht den jüdischen Geist nicht aus!* (München, 1991), 59–64. Discussion pertinent to the inner endangerment that comes with Christianity's becoming theological can also be found in the texts listed in note 19.

12. See first my contribution to the volume edited by E. Kogon and myself, *Gott nach Auschwitz* (Freiburg, 1979), 121–44; then consult "Facing the Jews: Christian Theology After Auschwitz," in *Faith and the Future*, 38–48. See also "The Church After Auschwitz," chap. 7, below. The radical significance of the catastrophe of Auschwitz for ecclesial and theological consciousness had already been pointed out in the document of the Synod of German Bishops, *Unsere Hoffnung: Ein Bekenntnis zum Glauben in dieser Zeit* (1975).

13. Besides chapter 10, see "Der Kampf um jüdische Traditionen in der christlichen Gottesrede," in *Kirche und Israel*

1987/1:14–23, and "Die Synagoge als Gotteslehrerin," in the *Festchrift* for Dorothee Sölle: Schottroff and Thiele (eds.), *Gotteslehrerinnen* (Stuttgart, 1989), 15–22.

14. See the texts listed in n. 2.

15. For my view of the relationship between political and liberation theologies, along with the foreword to the new (German) edition of Gutiérrez' *A Theology of Liberation* (see n. 4), see my "Thesen zum theologischen Ort der Befreiungstheologie," in J. B. Metz (ed.), *Die Theologie der Befreiung: Hoffnung oder Gefahr für die Kirche?* (Düsseldorf: 1987); also "Politische Theologie und die Herausforderung des Marxismus," in P. Rottländer (ed.), *Theologie der Befreiung und Marxismus* (Münster, 1987), 175–86; my introduction to J. B. Metz & P. Rottländer (eds.), *Lateinamerika und Europa* (München/Mainz, 1988); finally, the relevant passages from J. B. Metz & H.-E. Bahr, *Augen für die Anderen: Lateinamerika als theologische Erfahrung* (München, 1991).

16. On this issue see my contribution to *Zukunftsfähigkeit* as well as the continuation of those reflections in "Das Konzil—'der Anfang eines Anfangs'?"

17. See J. B. Metz, "Unity and Diversity: Problems and Prospects for Inculturation" in *Faith and the Future: Essays on Theology*, 57–65; see also "Die Eine Welt als Heausforderung an das westliche Christentum," in *Una Sancta*, 1989/4: 314–22.

18. See J. B. Metz, "1492—Through the Eyes of a European Theology," in *Faith and the Future*, 66–71.

19. See "Freedom in Solidarity," *Faith and the Future*, 72–78; also, "Geist Europas—Geist des Christentums," in P. Neuner & H. Wagner (eds.), *Verantwortung für den Glauben: Beiträge zur Fundamentaltheologie und Ökumene* (Freiburg, 1992).

20. See *Faith in History and Society*, 3–13.

21. *Biblical* monotheism must be understood not as something associated with power politics, but rather as a pathic monotheism, and must continually be protected against an almost constitutional, gnostic temptation to a dualism between salvation and time, between creation and redemption, that has

been present from its very beginnings. For a more detailed discussion of these themes, see "Theology versus Polymythicism: A Short Apology for Biblical Monotheism" (chap. 4, below); see also the relevant texts in "A Passion for God" (chap. 10, below) and, especially, in the theodicy text (chapter 3, below).

22. See above all "Die Verantwortung der Theologie in der Krise der Geisteswissenschaften" (n. 8) and the texts listed in n. 23.

23. Theodicy is not understood here in the sense of a rational justification of God, but rather in the sense of a question as to how we can talk about God at all in the face of the history of suffering in the world, in "his" world; see below, chap. 3. See "Plädoyer für mehr Theodizee-Empfindlichkeit in der Theologie," in W. Oelmüller (ed.), *Wovon man nicht schweigen kann: Neuere Diskussionen zur Theodizeefrage* (München, 1992). On a way of talking about God that is sensitive to theodicy in the world of the mass media, see "Was ist mit der Gottesrede geschehen?" in *Herder Korrespondenz*, September 1991, 418–22.

24. A central theological issue, which for the most part has been repressed in theology, is the theme of time; but all biblical statements about being, correctly understood, bear a temporal index. See "Theology versus Polymythicism" (chap. 4, below), and "Theologie gegen Mythologie" (n. 21). For a debate with Nietzsche on this issue, see (besides the two aforementioned texts) "Wohin ist Gott, wohin denn der Mensch" (n. 9), and—specifically on the theme of time—"Ohne Finale ins Nichts: Die Herrschaft der endlosen Zeit und die Angst" [in a slightly different form in "Time without a Finale," *Faith and the Future*, 79–86; Ed.].

2. ON THE WAY TO A POSTIDEALIST THEOLOGY

1. As is well known, this pair of concepts—paradigm and paradigm shift—was introduced into the history and philosophy of science by Thomas Kuhn, in *The Structure of Scientific Revolutions* (Chicago, IL: University of Chicago Press, 1962). However, I apply the concepts here only in the more general meanings they

have come to have in the disciplines of the so-called human sciences. They cannot be applied to theology and theological processes with the specific meanings they have in Kuhn's work.

2. The epoch here characterized as "modernity" did not begin with the religious and profane divisions of the sixteenth century—in the sense of the classical distinctions between antiquity, middle ages, and modernity. Rather, it began with the processes of the Enlightenment that have brought far-reaching transformations to the social-political and scientific worlds.

3. Joseph Kleutgen, *Die Theologie der Vorzeit* (Frankfurt am Main: Minerva, 1974).

4. Very briefly, the decisive criteria for a new paradigm in theology are these: (1) the capacity to perceive crises and to preserve tradition in nontraditionalistic ways in the face of those crises; (2) the power of concentration, both (a) the nonregressive reduction of overcomplexity and overspecialization that cause crises in theology to be hidden or repressed by division of labor, and (b) the nontrivial reduction of doctrine to life or doxography to biography, since the logos of theology always aims for some form of wisdom as a form of life; (3) the capacity and readiness to move back and forth between theological and ecclesial contexts, since there is no hermetically sealed history of crises in theology (they are always crises of the Christian subject and his or her praxis), and a paradigm shift in theology collapses into a vacuum if it is not accompanied by changes in ecclesial life or if theology does not take part in those changes and nourish itself from them.

5. I have already stressed in *Faith in History and Society* that it "should be of decisive importance that the problem of constituting theological reason be solved not simply on 'this side' of idealism, but rather to make the attempt to remain on 'the other side of idealism' and do theology there" (*my* translation, see *Glaube in Geschichte und Gesellschaft,* 50; cf. *Faith in History and Society,* 53).

6. On this fundamental "salvific" character of theology or of theological hermeneutics, see my interpretation of the "apologetic" nature of theology: *Faith in History and Society,* 5–8.

7. The usual ecclesial division of labor of which I speak here

may be described—perhaps too briefly—as follows: The bishops teach; the priests care for; the (professional) theologians explain and defend doctrine and train the caretakers. And the rest? The people? They are chiefly the objects of this instructing and caretaking church. The image of church that directs this division of labor is the image of a people's church as a caretaker church. And the theology which unquestioningly submits to this division of labor reproduces in its turn, *nolens volens*, this paternalistic system. Yet this image of the caretaker church is not the staightforwardly canonical one; today it is no longer universal and uncontested. Precisely for the sake of pastoral and missionary tasks, and for the sake of ecumenism, we find today a transition from a caretaker church for the people to a church of the people, that is to say, to a church with a growing base of and in subjects. Within this transition questions arise in a new way about the religious orders, and about the subjects and competency of the theological enterprise.

8. See *Faith in History and Society*, chap. 4. There I also stress that, for a postidealist theology, the idea of a God to which Christian theology is accountable is itself practical. It always disrupts the interests of those who try only to think it. The biblical stories of rebellion, of conversion, of resistance and of suffering belong to its "definition." The "pure" concept of God is the abbreviation, to a certain degree the shorthand version of the histories in terms of which theology must continually decipher its concepts. Therefore, saying that a postidealist theology has a narrative-practical character is not an arbitrary suggestion; this character belongs to its foundations. See "A transcendental and idealistic or a narrative and practical Christianity?" in *Faith in History and Society*, chap. 9.

9. On the latter, see the comments below in section III.

10. At this point a Christianity holding itself accountable to the idea of liberation becomes a critical challenge to Marxism. Christianity and Marxism are also differentiated in a corresponding way on the issue of violence. See *The Emergent Church*, 97–99. On the question of revolutionary consciousness and the

consciousness of guilt, see *The Emergent Church*, 104–6. On the relationship between theology and ethics, which has not yet been sufficiently developed in the new political theology, see Jürgen Moltmann's *Politische Theologie—Politische Ethik* (München, 1984).

11. This is true also for the psychological theories of development that are the rage today in systematic and pastoral theology; not even they are innocent as far as faith and theology go. They reinterpret the dangerous God of the Bible as a nice God of human self-realization, to whom I can quietly bid adieu once I have "found myself" and my "identity."

12. It is precisely this form of knowledge that theology has to represent and elaborate in terms of its communicative significance in interdisciplinary discourse among the sciences. See the description of the categories of memory and narrative, in their subjectwise and practical character, in *Faith in History and Society*, chaps. 11 and 12.

13. Synod Document, *Unsere Hoffnung*, I. 3.

14. See the comments in section III.

15. Once again, see the concluding comments in section III. See also the comments on the "struggle for lost time," *Faith in History and Society*, chap. 10.

16. I have tried to show in *Followers of Christ* (Mahwah, N.J.: Paulist Press, 1978) in what way it is precisely Jesus' passion that can be qualified as a suffering unto God, and how this is a thoroughly christological qualification.

17. In my essay, "In the Face of the Jews: Christian theology after Auschwitz," [in Metz & Moltmann, *Faith and the Future* (Maryknoll, N.Y.: Orbis, 1995), 38–48], I have tried to work out how and with what consequences this horror should be respected theologically. I start from the fact that it is necessary to defend the dignity of the nonidentity of human suffering, in contrast to a theology that discusses the horrors of the human histories of suffering under the constraints of identity-thinking. Here there is no language for theology without recourse to the language of suffering and the crisis of believing subjects themselves.

18. See above all *The Emergent Church* (New York: Crossroad, 1987), *passim.* [The German title of the original, *Jenseits bürgerlicher Religion* (Mainz: Matthias-Grünewald, 1980) is more literally translated, "Beyond Bourgeois Religion."—*Trans.*]

19. On this and on the fundamental features of a discipleship Christology, see the relevant passages in *Followers of Christ.* This Christology starts from the fact that in the New Testament there are various (albeit not mutually exclusive) ways of believing—above all, a synoptic and a Pauline way of believing. It is legitimate and extremely important today to bring into the foreground the synoptic way of believing, in which faith and discipleship are used more or less synonymously.

20. *Unsere Hoffnung,* III, 1.

21. See my comments in "Toward a Second Reformation," in *The Emergent Church,* 48–66.

22. Hence I am taking up and carrying on themes that I have published as "Untimely Theses on Apocalyptic." See, *Faith in History and Society,* chap. 10.

23. Ernst Bloch has already given this variant.

24. On this naiveté—as the capacity for a *productive noncontemporaneity*—see my essay, "Productive Noncontemporaneity," in Jürgen Habermas (ed.), *Observations on "the Spiritual Situation of the Age,"* translated with an introduction by Andrew Buchwalter (Cambridge, MA: MIT Press, 1984), 169–77.

25. [*Ärgernis* and *ärgern* are the noun and verb forms used in German to render "stumbling block" (e.g., Rom 14:13, 1 Cor 1:23) and "take offense" (e.g., Lk 7:23). I have translated them accordingly.—*Trans.*]

26. Has theology given enough attention to this sort of end to history—the theology which, after all, talks about a salvation in the flesh of this history? Are we able to address and comment on this problem at all anymore? Have we not neglected the very resources which would allow us to resist? For example, have we not in theology too quickly rejected the category of *narrative,* even though it is probably the only form in which time can still be discussed and conveyed as nonlinear time, as discontinuity

and interruption, in short, as history? Under the name of a practical fundamental theology, I have tried to make at least some initial attempts to place these and similar perspectives among the fundamental questions.

27. This representation of time is not (theologically speaking) innocent. It is not even merely agnostic, for example in the fashion of a methodological atheism. For it the eschatological God—the God of the living and of the dead, the God who touches even past suffering, who does not leave even the dead in their repose—is absolutely unthinkable. In it, much more than in any militant atheism, is found the really apathetic godlessness of modernity.

3. THEOLOGY AS THEODICY?

1. See Hans Blumenberg, *Säkularisierung und Selbstbehauptung* (Frankfurt, 1974), 155.

2. Karl Rahner, "Why Does God Allow Us to Suffer?", in *Theological Studies 19*, trans. Edward Quinn (New York: Crossroad, 1983), 195f. (translation slightly emended).

3. S. Kierkegaard, Pap. X 1 A 640 (=Tagebücher), dt. von H. Gerdes, Bd. III (Düsseldorf-Köln, 1968), 275.

4. F. König & R. Rahner (Hrsg.), *Europa: Horizonte der Hoffnung* (Graz-Wien-Köln, 1983), 68.

5. [On this translation see chap. 1, n. 10—*Ed.*]

6. [Nelly Sachs (1891–1970) was a German-born Swedish poet and dramatist and winner of the Nobel Prize for literature (1966). A Jew, she barely escaped the death camps by fleeing to Sweden in 1940, after which her poetry became a powerful witness to the suffering of the victims of the Holocaust. Her later poetry shows the strong influence of Hasidism in particular, and of elements of Jewish mysticism in general.—*Ed.*].

7. Elie Wiesel, *The Night Trilogy* (New York: Noonday Press, 1988), 15.

8. E. Biser, *Interpretation und Veränderung* (Paderborn, 1979), 132f.

9. *Der Gottesbegriff nach Auschwitz. Eine jüdische Stimme,* st. 1516 (Frankfurt, 1987).

10. For more details, see below, "Theology versus Polymythicism," chapter 4.

4. THEOLOGY VERSUS POLYMYTHICISM

1. In the sense of the Second Law of Thermodynamics, for example.

2. See above, all the recent works by Hans Blumenberg and the collection of essays edited by Odo Marquard, *Farewell to Matters of Principle* (Oxford: Oxford University Press, 1989). See also Hans Magnus Enzensberger, "Second Thoughts on Consistency," in *Political Crumbs,* trans. Martin Chalmers (New York: Verso, 1990), 1–15.

3. G. Krüger, "Die Bedeutung der Tradition für die philosophische Forschung," in *Studium Generale* 4 (1951), 322ff.

4. Walter Benjamin, "Anmerkungen der Herausgeber," in *Gesammelte Schriften,* II 3, Frankfurt, 1974, 1232.

5. For a critique of compensatory thinking see, for example, the "Diskussion über die These vom Ende der Modernität," in Koslowski, Spaemann, Löw (eds.), *Moderne oder Postmoderne* (Weinheim, 1986), 4 (remarks from the discussion between R. Spaemann and R. Maurer).

6. See *Faith in History and Society,* 65–67, 172–75.

7. *Ibid.,* 63f.

8. See chapter 2 above, pages 47–53.

9. See O. Marquard, *In Defense of the Accidental,* trans. Robert Wallace (NY: Oxford, 1991), *passim* (especially: universal history and multiversal history).

10. Jürgen Moltmann, *God in Creation: A new theology of creation and the Spirit of God* (San Francisco: Harper & Row, 1985), 107–8.

11. To use a formulation of H. Lübbe.

12. *Werke* (ed. Schlechta) III 534, 540, 903; 480 (*sämtl. Nachlaß*). In "Thus Spoke Zarathustra" Nietzsche pressed again and again, in various forms, this demand: "The person is something

which should be overcome, which must be overcome"; see *The Portable Nietzsche*, translated, edited and with an introduction by Walter Kaufmann (New York: Penguin Books, 1968), 121f., 149f., 160, 311, 379.

13. See his short work, "On Truth and Falsity in Their Ultramoral Sense," in Friedrich Nietzsche, *Early Greek Philosophy and Other Essays*, trans. Maximilian Mügge (New York: Russell and Russell, 1964), 173–92.

14. For example, Friedrich Nietzsche, *Daybreak*, trans. R. J. Hollingdale (Cambridge: Cambridge University Press), 108.

15. See Niklas Luhmann, *Ecological Communication*, trans. John Bednasz (Chicago: Univ. of Chicago Press, 1989).

16. On this formulation of Nietzsche's, as well as on the following quote, see Martin Heidegger, "Who Is Nietzsche's Zarathustra?" in *Nietzsche*, Vol. II, trans. David Farrell Krell (San Francisco: Harper and Row, 1979), 211–32.

17. *Ibid.*

18. *Ibid.*

19. Perhaps here it becomes clear why Christian theology, seen correctly, is *political theology*—not just fortuitously, but necessarily—and why that term in the Judaeo-Christian context is really a pleonasm. To be sure, it needs precisely because of this to be sounded out in more detail. The position represented here differs from Carl Schmitt's political theology at its very foundations, because of the latter's understanding of God and of monotheism. Indeed, it is closer to the position of Walter Benjamin, though, to be sure, only on a sundered shore.

20. Gerhard von Rad, *Old Testament Theology*, trans. D. M. G. Stalker (New York: Harper, 1962), I:398. See also the reference to the Egyptians in that book (with E. Otto): "We have learned from all the epochs of Egyptian history that the Egyptians loved to 'idealize' factual events." H. Jonas shared von Rad's judgment concerning Israel (see n. 25).

21. On this characterization of the Job-tradition, see J. Ebach, "Thesen zum Hiobbuch," in W. Oelmüller (Hrsg.), *Leiden* (*Kolloquien zur Gegenwartsphilosophie.* Paderborn, 1986), 20–27, esp. 27.

22. Karl Rahner, *Foundations of Christian Faith*, 446.

23. See J. B. Metz, *Faith in History and Society*, chap. 10, as well as the citations under "time" and "apocalyptic." J. Taubes represents in the philosophy of history and in eschatology the interpretation of time as "bounded period," although with a problematic inter-twining of apocalyptic and gnostic elements.

24. See the discussion cited in n. 23, as well as "The Dangerous Christ," in chap. 2, above, pages 47–53, and "Kampf um jüdische Traditionen in der christlichen Gottesrede," in *Kirche und Israel* 2 (1987):14–23, esp. 19ff. Jürgen Moltmann makes some crucial observations and distinctions concerning the formula "God's being is in coming, not in becoming" in his *God in Creation*, 124–39.

25. See H. Jonas, *Gnosis und spätantiker Geist* (Göttingen: 1954) I:12ff., 62ff.

26. Certainly it is not easy today to find discussions of this "mother of Christian theology" (Ernst Käsemann) that are unambivalent and free of ressentiment, not distorted by cur-rently fashionable attitudes. In systematic theology proper, apoca-lypticism has for the most part been proscribed in the name of a more congenial, existentially or evolutionistically colored eschatology. Correspondingly, it is fashionable to see apocalyptic as a free-floating metaphor one can explain without any further ado by pointing to mounting fears of catastrophe. In philosophy (perhaps for this very reason?) it has once again been subjected to the sharpest critique. Because of its attitudes of imminent expectation, it is supposed to be the attempt (always suspect of terroristic tendencies) to absorb the course of worldly time into the individual lifetime, which always ends catastrophically, and to poison the public sphere (which is already in danger anyway) with fantasies of decline and catastrophe. And in fact it is not easy to make out apocalypticism as a whole in terms of the imagi-native perception of the world that guides it. Late Jewish apoca-lypticism is an extremely complex and multileveled phenomenon. There are enough Persian-dualistic elements therein to see it as closely related to a world-denying Gnosticism,

as a sort of historical fatalism in sharp contrast to prophetic eschatology. But in the light of the historical genealogy of the concept of God in Israel, this apocalypticism appears not as a deviation, but much more as a culmination. See the essay cited under note 24 from *Kirche und Israel.*

27. See Jürgen Moltmann, *Theology of Hope* (New York: Harper & Row, 1967), 133ff., though of course Moltmann does not there start from the problematic of time itself.

28. The differences become clear in Paul's speech on the Areopagus (Acts 17, esp. v. 32).

29. Not even the so-called Johannine way of believing stands wholly under the spell of Gnosticism: see the works by H. Schlier and the essay by Louise Schottfroff, "Mein Reich ist nicht von dieser Welt: Der johanneische Messianismus," in J. Taubes (ed.), *Gnosis und Politik* (Paderborn: 1984), 97–108.

30. As I believe to be the case in Panneberg's universal history approach, an approach influenced by Hegel.

31. As in Teilhard de Chardin and, to a certain degree, even in Karl Rahner. See, for example, his "Christology within an evolutionary World-View," *Theological Investigations Volume V: Later Writings,* trans. Karl-H. Kruger (New York: Crossroad, 1983), 157–92.

32. As in Rudolf Bultmann's theology. On the gnostic-sounding myth of identity in Bultmann, see F. Schupp, "Mythos und Religion: Der Spielraum der Ordnung," in H. Poser (ed.), *Philosphie und Mythos* (Berlin, 1979), 72.

33. As I think is still true of Moltmann and Jüngel. See my comments in *Faith in History and Society,* 130–33, and in "On the Way to a Postidealist Theology," above, p. 42.

34. See G. Lohfink, *Zur Möglichkeit christlicher Naherwartung,* in Greshake/Lohfink, *Naherwartung—Auferstehung—Unsterblichkeit* (Freiburg, 1975), 53f.

35. See my reference to Beckett's "Waiting for Godot" in *Faith in History and Society,* 170.

36. Thus, for example, even Lohfink—despite his energetic retrieval of this topos (see n. 34).

37. See J. Taubes, *Das stählerne Gehäuse und der Exodus oder Ein Streit um Marcion, einst und heute*, in Taubes (ed.), *Gnosis und Politik*, 9–15. Even earlier we find something quite similar in Ernst Bloch, *Atheism in Christianity*, 194.

38. As, for example, Aland has clearly shown in "Was ist Gnosis? Wie wurde sie überwunden? Versuch einer Kurzdefinition," in *Gnosis und Politik*, 54–65.

39. Here I am following the incisive account given by Jürgen Moltmann in *The Theology of Hope*, 56–57.

40. Since—and this has to be conceded to Hans Blumenberg—even the Middle Ages (with its doctrine of analogy) does not represent a definitive victory over Gnosticism.

41. In this context my own category of *interruption* (from Walter Benjamin) needs further testing. In my view it would be just as worthwhile to confront Ernst Bloch's noncontemporaneity-thesis with a genuinely theological concept of time (see J. B. Metz, "Productive Noncontemporaneity" in Habermas, ed., *Observations on "the Spiritual Situation of the Age"*: *Contemporary German Perspectives*, trans. Andrew Buchwalter (Cambridge, MA: MIT Press, 1984), 169–77. On Bloch's noncontemporaneity-thesis, see B. Schmidt, *Postmoderne—Strategien des Vergessens, Sammlung Luchterhand* 606, 1986.

42. See "New Testament and Mythology," in Rudolf Bultmann, *New Testament and Mythology, and Other Basic Writings*, trans. and ed. by Schubert Ogden (Philadelphia: Fortress Press, 1984), 5 [translation slightly emended].

43. See in this regard Max Horkheimer's remark at the Salzburg humanism debate: Theology is always carrying on a liberalizing paralysis of Christianity, as it "attempts to adapt itself to societal...notions of time, so that it does not have to require of people anything which today could not but seem comical or strange." [From: *Hat die Religion Zukunft?* Graz, 1971, 117; also, Karl Löwith's observations, *ibid.*, 319].

44. Following H. Otto's citation in *Was heißt Wiederkunft Christi?*, 78. P. Schütz's position, which stresses so emphatically the idea of the second coming, seems to me to be explicitly gnos-

tic: for him the "second coming" is an "image" for illuminating the confrontation between God and world. See the text just cited.

45. See Karl Rahner & Herbert Vorgrimler, *Theological Dictionary*, ed. by Cornelius Ernst and trans. by Richard Strachan (New York: Herder & Herder, 1965), 336.

46. To be sure, the question of how one remains true to the understanding of imminent expectation and second coming is also a thoroughly practical-critical question for the church and the ecclesial regime. Dostoevsky's story of the grand inquisitor depicts a church which, in its officeholders, has long ago dismissed the idea of a second coming, although it is always on their lips. It should not be assumed that considerations presented here move only at speculative heights, without having implications for Christianity and the church as they exist in the concrete. See the questions placed against the horizon of bounded time for ecclesial life in J. B. Metz, *Followers of Christ*.

47. See my comments relevant to the following in F. X. Kaufmann, J. B. Metz, *Zukunftsfähigkeit: Suchbewegungen im Christentum*.

48. See Hans Magnus Enzensberger, "Reluctant Eurocentrism: A Political Picture Puzzle" in *Political Crumbs*, 17–33.

5. DO WE MISS KARL RAHNER?

1. Karl Rahner, *The Shape of the Church to Come*, translated with an introduction by Edward Quinn (New York: Crossroad, 1983).

2. *The Shape of the Church to Come*, 66f. (translation slightly emended).

3. *Ibid.*, 69f.

4. Karl Rahner, *The Shape of the Church to Come*, 104f. (my own translation—*Ed.*).

5. Karl Rahner, "A Dream of the Church," in *Concern for the Church: Theological Investigations XX*, 133–42; Heinrich Fries & Karl Rahner, *Unity of the Churches—An Actual Possibility*, translated

by Ruth C. L. Gritsch & Eric W. Gritsch (Philadelphia: Fortress Press; New York: Paulist Press, 1985).

6. KARL RAHNER'S STRUGGLE FOR THE THEOLOGICAL DIGNITY OF HUMANKIND

1. See *Schriften zur Theologie* (Einsiedeln: Benziger, 1960), volume 8 and especially volume 14. [Volume 8 in *Schriften zur Theologie* is translated as volumes 9 and 10 of *Theological Investigations* (New York: Crossroad, 1973); volume 14 is translated as volumes 19 and 20 (1976).—*Trans.*]

2. [Aptitude is used here to translate *Begabung*, which can also be translated as talent, skill or gift, as in "a gift for the violin."—*Trans.*]

3. *Theological Investigations 13*, 66f.

4. See, *Faith in History and Society*, chap. 9.

5. See *Theological Investigations 19*, 194–208.

6. *Ibid.*, 195f.

7. *Ibid.*, 208.

8. *Theological Investigations 22*, 165ff.

9. *Ibid.*, 173.

10. Only in this way, as he returns to the question of God, is Rahner a universalist of salvation and of reconciliation. Thus, with his virtually mystical trust in the universal salvific will of God, he does not represent any sort of theologically perspicuous universal reconciliation that would present to men and women evidence of their ultimate innocence concerning all their deeds and consequently defuse the drama of human freedom.

11. Karl Rahner, *Karl Rahner in Dialogue: Conversations and Interviews, 1965–1982* (New York: Crossroad, 1986), 126f.

7. THE CHURCH AFTER AUSCHWITZ

1. [*Heimatrecht*, or "right of residence," is a technical term for the legal right of Jews to live in a given region. Unlike other residents, Jews were not guaranteed this right simply by being born

in the region. Rather, up until the end of the eighteenth century, this right had to be negotiated and paid for by the Jewish community.—*Ed.*]

2. Johann Gottlieb Fichte, *Beiträge zur Berichtigung der Urtheile des Publicums über die Französische Revolution,* in J. H. Fichte (ed.), *Johann Gottlieb Fichte's sämmtliche Werke* (Berlin, 1845–46), vol. VI, p. 150.

8. THEOLOGY AND THE UNIVERSITY

1. I owe this phrase to Peter Rottländer.

9. MONOTHEISM AND DEMOCRACY

1. See H. Dubiel, *Ungewißheit und Politik* (Frankfurt, 1994), 93; R. Dahrendorf, "Freiheit und soziale Bindungen: Anmerkungen zur Struktur einer Argumentation," in K. Michalski (ed.), *Die liberale Gesellschaft* (Stuttgart, 1993), 11–20.

2. F. Nietzsche, *Werke,* 16-bändige Groß- und Kleinoktavausgabe, 10:289.

3. *Ungewißheit und Politik,* 178.

4. *Riskante Freiheiten: Individualisierung in modernen Gesellschaften,* ed. v. U. Beck & E. Beck-Gernsheim (Frankfurt, 1994).

5. As in his contribution "Philosophie und Engagement," in the *Frankfurter Rundschau,* May 15, 1995.

6. Here I am using "Anmerkungen zu Hannah Arendts politischer Theorie," in H. Dubiel's work (see n. 1).

7. Alexis de Tocqueville, *Democracy in America,* trans. George Lawrence (Garden City, NY: Doubleday, 1969), 294.

8. Robert Bellah, et al., *Habits of the Heart* (San Francisco: Harper Torch, 1985).

9. On this loss of substance in the concept of religion in North America, see O. Kallsheuer, *Individuum, Gemeinschaft und die Seele Amerikas,* in *Transit* 5 (1992–93), 31–50, esp. 40ff. For a more detailed account, see also Catherine Albanese, *America:*

Religion and Religions, 2nd ed. (Belmont, CA: Wadsworth Publishing Co., 1992), 419ff.

10. I take this brief characterization from J. Moltmann; see his essay "Protestantism as a 'religion of freedom'," in Jürgen Moltmann (ed.), *Religion der Freiheit* (München, 1990), 11–28.

11. A. Heller, "Politik nach dem Tod Gottes," in J. Huber & A. M. Müller (eds.), *Instanzen/Perspektiven/Imaginationen* (Zürich, 1995), 75–94. This quote is on 94. On the metaphysical background to the political concept of modernity, see 82.

12. On this position in contemporary political philosophy in France, see W. van Reijen, "Das politische Denken," in *Transit 5* (Winter 1992/93), 109–22.

13. See, for example, R. Dahrendorf (op cit, n. 1).

14. Immanuel Kant, "What Is Enlightenment?" in *Immanuel Kant: Philosophical Writings*, Ernst Behler, ed. (New York: Continuum, 1986), 264.

15. See for example J. B. Metz, "Wider die zweite Unmündigkeit: Zum Verhältnis von Aufklärung und Christentum," in Rüsen, Lämmert & Glotz (eds.), *Die Zukunft der Aufklärung* (Frankfurt, 1988), 81–87.

16. See, "Anamnestic Reason: A Theologian's Remarks on the Crisis in the *Geisteswissenschaften*," in *Cultural-Political Interventions in the Unfinished Project of Enlightenment*, ed. Thomas McCarthy et al. (Cambridge, MA: MIT Press, 1992), 189–94. Why is it that the catastrophe of Auschwitz does not show up in Habermas' major theoretical works, but only in his *Kleine politische Schriften* (see vols. V–VIII, Frankfurt: Suhrkamp, 1985–1995 [some essays found in vols. V & VI have been translated in *The New Conservatism: Cultural Criticism and the Historians' Debate* (Cambridge, MA.: MIT Press, 1989)—*Ed.*])—although here, as we all know, in a way that is just as decisive as it is influential. After Auschwitz, can one in fact still ignore the consequences of distinguishing the anamnestic from communicative reason and exercise a mutual disregard in this way? Or is this not precisely an indication that communicative reason has not taken anamnestic reason into itself, even though this is exactly what

Habermas asserted with regard to my critique—see J. Habermas, "Israel und Athen, oder: Wem gehört anamnetische Vernunft?" in *Diagnosen der Zeit* (Düsseldorf, 1994), 51–64.

17. Erik Peterson, *"Der Monotheismus als politisches Problem,"* in his *Theologische Traktate* (München, 1951), 45–147.

18. On this "pathic monotheism" see Tiemo Peters, *Conversio ad Passionem,* in Engel-Eggensperger (ed.), *Wahrheit: Recherchen zwischen Hoschscholastik und Postmoderne* (Mainz, 1995). From my own works, see "Theology versus Polymythicism" (above, chap. 4), "Die Rede von Gott angesichts der Leidensgeschichte der Welt, in *Stimmen der Zeit* 210 (1992), 311–20; "Gotteskrise: Versuch zur 'geistigen Situation der Zeit'," in *Diagnosen zur Zeit* (Düsseldorf: 1994), 76–92. For a more detailed definition of the relationship between the Christian *memoria passionis* and the *memoria resurrectionis,* see above all the essay in *Stimmen der Zeit.*

19. The universalism (of suffering) being asserted here is a "negative universalism"; as such it can be formulated without myth or ideology on modernity's ground. The problem that still remains is how to qualify this negative universalism by means of the (positive) concept of justice, or by talk about unjust suffering. I will only join in the discussion of the question of justice again after I have learned how to overcome the purely procedural way of dealing with this question.

20. Someone who starts from the fact that situations of suffering can never be wholly abolished is in no way asserting thereby that they cannot and must not be changed; for not everything that cannot be abolished is also unchangeable.

21. This is Peter Rottländer's formulation.

22. The present discussions on the theme of liberalism show, in my view, how legitimate the suspicion is that classical liberalism has developed only a restricted social sensitivity—precisely in view of global problems and conflicts (North-South!).

23. Carl Schmitt, *The Concept of the Political,* trans. George Schwab (New Brunswick, NJ: Rutgers University Press, 1976), 54; the German text dates from 1932, and has a foreword and three appendices.

24. H. M. Enzensberger, *Aussichten auf den Bürgerkrieg* (Frankfurt, 1994), 74.

25. *Ibid.*, 19.

26. For aporetic formulations of the indispensability of tradition one could consult positions as varied as those of Theodor Adorno, Leszek Kolakowski, Hermann Lübbe and Willi Oelmüller. Talk of "appropriating the Semantic potential of the past" (especially of biblical-monotheistic traditions) as it is found in Jürgen Habermas (in, for instance, *Postmetaphysical Thinking: Philosophical Essays*, trans. W. M. Hohengarten [Cambridge, MA: MIT Press, 1992], 15) would require a more detailed discussion—and not least in connection with Habermas' talk of a decidedly posttraditionalist society.

27. See note 1.

28. *Riskante Freiheiten* (n. 4), 431.

29. Dubiel, (n. 1), 149.

10. A PASSION FOR GOD: RELIGIOUS ORDERS TODAY

1. [*Zeit der Orden? Zur Mystik und Politik der Nachfolge* (Freiburg: Herder, 1977). Literally translated, the title is "A Time for the Orders? On the Mysticism and Politics of Discipleship." The English translation is *Followers of Christ: The Religious Life and the Church*, trans. Thomas Linton (New York: Paulist Press, 1978.—Trans.]

2. *Followers of Christ*, 7–8. [The council to which Metz refers is the Second Vatican Council; the synod is the Synod of West German Bishops, for which he served as theological consultant from 1971 to 1975.—Ed.]

3. *Ibid.*, 13.

4. *Ibid.*, 11–26.

5. *Søren Kierkegaard's Journals and Papers*, vol. 3, edited and translated by Howard Hung and Edna Hung (Bloomington, IN: University of Indiana Press, 1975), 84–85.

6. Friedrich Nietzsche, *The Gay Science; with a Prelude in*

rhymes and an appendix of songs, trans. Walter Kaufmann (New York: Vintage Books, 1974), Book III, no. 125 (pp. 181-82).

7. Here we would need a more detailed analysis of how literalism is not identical with the fundamentalism that is to be found today throughout the world (in virtually every religion and culture), and which, with its own way of rejecting discourse and hermeneutics, disenfranchises both religiously and politically those who think differently or are resisting. This fundamentalism, which follows the global processes of modernization and secularization like a shadow (and thus indirectly points out their inner contradictions), is in my view less a phenomenon of *radicalization* (in its etymological sense) than it is an attempt to compensate for the plurality and diffuseness of our modern life-worlds.

8. Odo Marquard used this metaphor to describe the situation and function of the philosopher in our scientific world. I think it lends itself even more to a condensed description of the relationship between monasticism and Christianity, between the church of the religious orders and the larger church.

9. See *Followers of Christ*, 62 [translation emended].

10. On the God-question in the horizon of the theodicy question, therefore in the face of the world's history of suffering, see "Theology as Theodicy?", chap. 3 above.

11. See *Followers of Christ*, 47–71.

12. [I follow the German citations given by Metz from the *Einheitsübersetzung*—Ed.]

13. *Poverty of Spirit*, trans. John Drury (New York: Paulist Press, 1968).

14. The following considerations gather up the whole pre-Christian biblical history under this proposition: Israel was incapable of letting itself be consoled by myths. See also the discussion in chaps. 4 and 6.

15. What later comes to be called biblical monotheism is rooted in Israel's passion for God. Right now this monotheism is weathering the sharpest critiques. For many it is an ideology of domination; it is seen as a cause for a predemocratic, antiegali-

tarian mentality centered around notions of sovereignty, as a source for obsolete patriarchy and political fundamentalism. Nietzsche, for his part, talked about the "pitiable God of Christian monotono-theism." And ever since, even Christian theology has frequently kept its distance from this biblical monotheism. It tries, for example by means of depth psychology, to get behind it to a polymythic primordial history of humanity, or—with themes from trinitarian theology—tries to see through it and resolve it into an inner-divine history.

In my view, of course, such attempts are finally nothing other than the theological mirroring of the polytheistically and polymythically colored atmosphere of our so-called postmodern world. At any rate the biblical system is not a system at all, correctly understood, but rather an event, an eschatological event. As such it is not a monotheism of power politics, but rather more a pathic monotheism with a painfully open eschatological flank. This distinguishes it from all nonbiblical monotheisms.

16. Following a saying of Nelly Sachs [see chap. 3, n. 6—*Ed.*].

17. The negative theology that comes to light here in the understanding of being poor before God, the proscription of images being taken seriously here, cuts short every attempt to make of the God of the biblical message a *convenient* God. As a woman said to me not long ago after a lecture by her therapist, "With his [the therapist's] help I have found an image of God that I can finally feel happy with." Of course it is not only much of psychology, but also church proclamations that like to serve up convenient images of God, in this case particularly those images of God that are convenient for the church's officeholders or preachers.

Why, for example, in the face of the situations of suffering in the world, are the official pronouncements of the church focused so much on human guilt (particularly in the sexual sphere) and so little on God's "guilt" regarding conditions in God's creation that cry out to heaven? Does not the church in its moral preaching stand here too much on the side of Job's friends and too little on the side of Job himself, who believed that faith was also capable of turning its questioning passionately back toward God? Did Jesus silence such questioning, or did he not in fact intensify it even more?

18. Theodor W. Adorno, *Kierkegaard: Construction of the Aesthetic*, trans. Robert Hullot-Kentor (Minneapolis: University of Minnesota Press, 1989), 141.

19. On this theme, see my discussion with Dorothee Sölle in *Welches Christentum hat Zukunft?* (Stuttgart, 1990).

20. From J. B. Metz, *Den Glauben lernen und lehren. Dank an Karl Rahner* (München, 1984), 24f.

21. *Becoming a subject* is a part of the fundamental program of the new political theology (see, for example, my book, *Faith in History and Society*). This understanding of the subject—and the way of speaking of the self in theology that corresponds to it—is founded in an *anamnestic anthropology*, in an anthropology of memory in which the subject finds him- or herself in the presence of others, with others (the living, far and near, as well as the dead, the vanquished and the victims), and only thus comes to know him- or herself in depth as a self. For even when I am thinking wholly and totally of my self, it never is a matter of myself alone. The political self is to be distinguished from the idealist self in theology (timeless, with no destiny, the same in all subjects); from the interpersonal self (which finds itself through the other Thou); and finally from the self of depth psychology, to the extent that this self grasps itself in its identity prior to others and without others—which can be seen, for example, in the therapeutic maxims that only a self already at peace with itself can come to peace with others, or that only a self that has already accepted itself can also accept others (as others).

On an anamnestically founded anthropology, see "Anamnestic Reason: A Theologian's Remarks on the Crisis in the *Geisteswissenschaften*" in *Cultural-Political Interventions in the Unfinished Project of Enlightenment*," A. Honneth, T. McCarthy, et al., eds. (Cambridge, MA: MIT Press, 1992), 189–94; my text on the crisis of the humanities in H. P. Müller, *Verantwortung des*

Wissens (Stuttgart, 1990); also the material in chapters 3, 4 and 6 above.

22. To be sure, such a hope is needy, since it can only be lived together with others, in the presence of others who also have learned or should learn to hope differently (absolutely not: for something different!). But it is only this dependency and neediness that guarantee the living and attractive diversity in the world of faith and overcome the typical, poorly informed stereotypes found in most faith-statements. It is precisely the constitutional being-with-others that makes it possible to say "I" authentically, even in theology. That is the way I have tried to formulate my own theology, very much from my own experience, which from the beginning denied me the possibility of understanding hope as a kind of naturally spontaneous confidence: very early on—in my experiences of the war as a youth, confronted with the dead faces of so many others—my childhood dreams, a sense of more or less harmonious normality for my life, fell apart. Instead, a whiff of uneasiness and lack of complete reconciliation—to some extent a particular sensitivity for theodicy, the conjuncture of hope and danger, and so on—accompanied my theological work from the very start. See in this regard, for example, the biographical references in my book with Dorothee Sölle, *Welches Christentum hat Zukunft?*

23. On this issue I refer you (although not entirely without reservations) to W. D. Rehfus, *Die Vernunft frißt ihre Kinder: Zeitgeist und Zerfall des modernen Weltbildes* (Hamburg: Hoffmann and Campe, 1990).

24. See sections V and VI.

25. On this issue, see the relevant texts in my contribution to F. X. Kaufmann, J. B. Metz, *Zukunftsfähigkeit: Suchbewegungen im Christentum* (Freiburg i.Br., 1987).

26. Besides *Zukunftsfähigkeit*, see "Die Eine Welt als Herausforderung an das westliche Christentum," *Una Sancta* 4/1989, 314–22; and "Unity and Diversity: Problems and Prospects for Inculturation" in J. Moltmann and J. B. Metz, *Faith and the*

Future: Essays on Theology, Solidarity and Modernity (Concilium Foundation/Orbis, 1995), 57–65.

27. Francis Fukuyama, *The End of History and the Last Man* (New York: Free Press, 1992).

28. On the relationship between Christianity and Europe, see the two texts "Krise der Geisteswissenschaften" and "Rettung der Vernunft."

29. [*"Volkskirchlichen"* refers to the traditional organizational and pastoral strategies of the European church, in which territorial parishes are inextricably woven into the cultural and social life of the people. Metz typically contrasts it with civil religion (*bürgerliche Religion*), which is the conscious or unconscious response, both theological and pastoral, to the new conditions in secularized, highly industrial societies. In the United States, civil religion might instead be called *liberal* or *progressive* religion.—*Ed.*)

30. See *Followers of Christ*, 15f.

31. Think of the "Jerusalem-communities" of Fr. Delfieux (for more details, see *Herder-Korrespondenz*, Feb. 1990).

32. Friedrich Nietzsche, *On the Genealogy of Morals* and *Ecce Homo*, translated by Walter Kaufmann and R. J. Hollingdale, edited with commentary by Walter Kaufmann (New York: Vintage Books, 1967), 326.

33. Symptoms of the death of man (as a subject) are given in the texts listed in n. 21, as well as in "Wohin ist Gott, wohin denn der Mensch? (from *Zukunftsfähigkeit*).

34. On "apocalypticism" without zealously heightened fantasies of catastrophe, but rather as an outline of life and the world against the horizon of bounded time, see chapter 4.

Sources

Chapter 1: "Vorwort zur 5. Auflage," *Glaube in Geschichte und Gesellschaft: Studien zu einer praktischen Fundamentaltheologie,* 5. Aufl. (Mainz: Matthias-Grünewald, 1992), 9–16.

Chapter 2: "Unterwegs zu einer nachidealistichen Theologie," in Johannes B. Bauer (ed.), *Entwürfe der Theologie* (Köln: Verlag Styria, 1985), 209–33.

Chapter 3: "Theologie als Theodizee" in Willi Oelmüller, ed., *Theodizee: Gott vor Gericht* (München: Wilhelm Fink, 1990), 103–18. This article is dedicated by Metz "for Willi Oelmüller on his birthday, 16 February, 1990."

Chapter 4: "Theologie versus Polymythie oder kleine Apologie des biblischen Monotheismus," in Odo Marquard (ed.), *Einheit und Vielheit: XIV Deutscher Kongreß für Philosophie* (Hamburg: Felix Meiner, 1990), 170–86.

Chapter 5: "Fehlt uns Karl Rahner?" in *Freiburger Akademiearbeiten: 1979–1989,* ed. Dietmar Bader, 527–39.

Chapter 6: "Karl Rahners Ringen um die theologische Ehre des Menschen," *Stimmen der Zeit* 212/6 (June, 1994), 383–92.

Chapter 7: From *Kirche nach Auschwitz: mit einem Anhang: für eine anamnetische Kultur* (Hamburg: Katholische Akademie Hamburg, 1993), 5–17.

Chapter 8: Response given by Professor Metz on the occasion of his receiving an honorary degree at the University of Vienna, December 15, 1995.

Chapter 9: Version of a lecture given originally at a 1995 meeting of the Austrian *Wissenschaftstag* on the theme of liberalism and democracy.

Chapter 10: From Johann Baptist Metz and Tiemo Rainer Peters, *Gottespassion: Zur Ordensexistenz heute* (Freiburg: Verlag Herder, 1991), 7–9, 13–62.

Bibliography

While not an exhaustive listing, the following is intended as a guide for further reading in Metz's thought. I have included all his work I know to be available in English. Only those German works are included that are necessary to give some idea of the breadth of Metz's thought over the past three and a half decades. Where both German and English texts of a work are given, it is because the English translation is somewhat different from the German original or is flawed.

A. ARTICLES IN LEXICONS AND ENCYCLOPEDIAS

In *Handbuch theologischer Grundbegriffe.* 2 vols. Edited by Heinrich Fries. München: Kösel Verlag, 1962:
"Freiheit," 1:403–14;
"Konkupiszenz," 1:843–51;
"Leiblichkeit," 2:29–37.

In *Lexicon für Theologie und Kirche.* 10 vols. Edited by Karl Rahner. Freiburg: Herder, 1957–65:
"Gespräch," 2:836–37;
"Leib," 6:902–05;
"Mitsein," 7:492–93;
"Theologie," 10:62–71;
"Unglaube," 10:496–99;
"Welt," 10:1023–26.

In *Mysterium Salutis: Grundriss heilsgeschichtlicher Dogmatik,* ed.
Johannes Feiner & Magnus Löhrer. Benziger, 1967:
Johann Baptist Metz with Francis Fiorenza. "Der Mensch als
Einheit von Leib und Seele."

In *Sacramentum Mundi.* 4 vols. Edited by Karl Rahner. Freiburg:
Herder, 1967–69:
"Apologetik," 1:266–76;
"Politische Theologie," 3:1232–40.

B. BOOKS, ARTICLES AND ADDRESSES

"Heidegger und das Problem der Metaphysik." In *Scholastik,* 28
(1953): 1–22.

"Theologische und Metaphysische Ordnung." In *Zeitschrift für
katolische Theologie* 83 (1961): 1–14. "The Theological World
and the Metaphysical World," trans. Dominic Gerlach. *Philosophy Today* 10/4 (Winter 1966).

Christliche Anthropozentrik: Uber die Denkform des Thomas von Aquin.
München: Kosel-Verlag, 1962.

"Freiheit als theologische-philosophische Grenzproblem." In
Gott in Welt: Festgabe für Karl Rahner, ed. J. B. Metz, et al.
Freiburg: Herder, 1964. "Freedom as a Threshold Problem
between Philosophy and Theology," trans. William J. Kramer.
Philosophy Today 10/4 (Winter 1966).

"Gott vor uns statt eines theologisches Argument." In *Ernst Bloch
zu ehren,* ed. Siegfried Unself. Frankfurt: Suhrkamp, 1965.

"The Controversy about the Future of Man: An Answer to Roger
Garaudy." *Journal of Ecumenical Studies* 4/2 (1967): 223–34.

Poverty of Spirit. Trans. John Drury. New York: Newman Press,
1968.

Zur Theologie der Welt. Mainz: Matthias-Grünwald Verlag, 1968.

Theology of the World, trans. William Glen-Doepel. New York: Herder and Herder, 1969 [English translation, with some changes and omissions, of *Zur Theologie der Welt*].

"'Politische Theologie' in der Diskussion." In *Diskussion zur "Politischen Theologie",* ed. Helmut Peukert. Mainz: Matthias-Grünewald, 1968.

"Prophetic Authority." In Metz, Moltmann and Oelmüller, *Religion and Political Society,* trans. and ed. by the Institute of Christian Thought. New York: Harper Forum Books, 1974.

"Zu Einer interdisziplinar orientierten Theologie auf bikonfessioneller Basis." In *Die Theologie in der interdisziplinaren Forschung,* ed. by J. B. Metz and T. Rendtorff. Düselldorf: Berteslmann Universistätsverlag, 1971.

Glaube in Geschichte und Gesellschaft, 1st-5th editions. Mainz: Matthias-Grünwald, 1977–92.

Faith in History and Society: Toward a Practical Fundamental Theology, translated by David Smith. New York: Seabury, 1980 [a very uneven translation of the second edition of *Glaube in Geschichte und Gesellschaft*].

"Vergebung der Sünden." *Stimmen der Zeit* 195/2 (Feb., 1977): 119–28.

Followers of Christ. Trans. by Thomas Linton. New York: Paulist Press, 1978.

Metz, Johann Baptist, with Karl Rahner. *The Courage to Pray.* Trans. by Sarah O'Brien Twohig. London: Search Press, 1980.

Unterbrechungen. Gütersloh: Gütersloher Verlagshaus, 1981.

"Productive Noncontemporaneity." In *Observations on "The Spiri-*

tual Situation of the Age," ed. Jürgen Habermas, trans. with an introduction by Andrew Buchwalter. Cambridge: MIT Press, 1984.

"Politische Theologie und die Herausforderung des Marxismus: Ein Gespräch des Herausgebers mit Johann Baptist Metz." In *Theologie der Befreiung und Marxismus*, ed. Peter Rottländer. München: edition liberación, 1986.

The Emergent Church. Trans. by Peter Mann. New York: Crossroad, 1987.

"Communicating a Dangerous Memory." In *Communicating a Dangerous Memory: Soundings in Political Theology*, ed. Fred Lawrence. Atlanta: Scholar's Press, 1987.

Metz, J. B., with F. X. Kaufmann, *Zukunftsfähigkeit: Suchbewegungen im Christentum*. Freiburg: Herder, 1987.

"Wider die zweite Unmündigkeit: Zum Verhältnis von Aufklärung und Christentum." In *Die Zukunft der Aufklärung*, ed. Rüssen, Lämmert, Glotz. Frankfurt: Suhrkamp, 1988.

"Theology in the New Paradigm: Political Theology." In *Paradigm Change in Theology*, ed. Hans Küng and David Tracy. New York: Crossroad, 1989.

"Theology in the Struggle for History and Society." Trans. by Dinah Livingstone. In *The Future of Liberation Theology: Essays in Honor of Gustavo Gutiérrez*, ed. M. Ellis & O. Maduro. New York: Orbis, 1989.

"Das Konzil—der Anfang eines Anfangs?" *Orientierung* 54/22 (November, 1990): 245–50.

"Die Verantwortung der Theologie in der gegenwärtigen Krise der Geisteswissenschaften." In *Wissen als Verantwortung: Ethische Konsequenzen des Erkennens*, ed. Hans-Peter Müller. Stuttgart: Kohlhammer, 1991.

Metz, Johann Baptist, with Dorothee Sölle. *Welches Christentum Hat Zukunft? Dorothee Sölle und Johann Baptist Metz im Gespräch mit Karl-Josef Kuschel.* Stuttgart: Kreuz Verlag, 1990.

Metz, Johann Baptist, with Tiemo Peters. *Gottespassion: Zur Ordensexistenz Heute.* Freiburg: Herder, 1991.

Metz, Johann Baptist, with H. E. Bahr. *Augen für die Anderen: Lateinamerika—eine theologische Erfahrung.* München: Kindler, 1991.

"Anamnestic Reason: A Theologian's Remarks on the Crisis in the *Geisteswissenschaften.*" In *Cultural-Political Interventions in the Unifnished Project of Enlightenment,* ed. Thomas McCarthy, et al. Cambridge, MA: MIT Press, 1992.

Trotzdem Hoffen: Mit Johann Baptist Metz und Elie Wiesel in Gespräch, Ekkehard Schuster & Reinhold Boschert-Kimmig (interviewers). Mainz: Matthias-Grünewald, 1993.

"Suffering Unto God," translated by J. Matthew Ashley. In *Critical Inquiry* 20/4 (Summer, 1994), 611–22.

Metz, Johann Baptist, with Jürgen Moltmann, *Faith and the Future: Essays on Theology, Solidarity, and Modernity,* with an Introduction by Francis Schüssler Fiorenza. Maryknoll, N.Y.: 1995 [collects the most important of Metz's essays from the journal *Concilium*].

"The Last Universalists." In *The Future of Theology: Essays in Honor of Jürgen Moltmann,* ed. Miroslav Volf, Carmen Krieg, and Thomas Kucharz. Grand Rapids, Mich.: Eerdmans, 1996.

C. SELECTED WORKS IN ENGLISH ON METZ

Ashley, J. Matthew. *Interruptions: Mysticism, Politics and Theology in the Work of Johann Baptist Metz.* Forthcoming from University of Notre Dame Press.

Chopp, Rebecca. *The Praxis of Suffering: An Interpretation of Liberation and Political Theologies.* Maryknoll: Orbis, 1986.

Colombo, Joseph. *An Essay on Theology and History: Studies in Pannenberg, Metz, and the Frankfurt School.* Atlanta: Scholars Press, 1990.

Guenther, Titus. *Rahner and Metz: Transcendental Theology as Political Theology.* New York: University Press of America, 1994.

Johns, Roger. *Man in the World: The Political Theology of Johannes Baptist Metz.* Atlanta: Scholars Press, 1976.

Ostovich, Steven. *Reason in History: Theology and Science as Community Activities.* Scholars Press: 1990.